annah; Georgia in ruins

ta, were engaged with other Union
n Tennessee. Only cavalry remained
rgia to harrass Sherman.

Union soldiers destroyed cotton
warehouses and railroads as they
They also destroyed crops and
ck.

Before leaving Atlanta, Sherman ordered the inhabitants out of the city and
set it on fire. To one who criticized him
for his destruction, he replied, "War is hell."

Sherman is expected now to move
northward through South Carolina when
he leaves Savannah.

wagon train near Fayetteville, Ga., on their march through Georgia.

Charged With Treason

To Fred and Barbara
From Michael P. H

011792

Other works

The Left Flank (1984)
After the Left Flank (1985)
"Roswell Past and Present" (1986)
"Cemetary Records of Roswell, Ga." (1988)
*The History of Law Enforcement in the Roswell
  Area, 1791-1990* (1990)

Michael D. Hitt

Charged With Treason:

Ordeal of 400 mill workers during
military operations in Roswell, Georgia,
1864-1865

Library Research Associates, Inc.
Monroe, New York
1992

Library Research Associates, Inc.
Dunderberg Road, RD#5, Box 41
Monroe, New York 10950

Cataloging-in-Publication Data

Hitt, Michael D., 1956-
    Charged with treason: ordeal of 400 mill workers during military operations
in Roswell, Georgia, 1864-1865/Michael D. Hitt.
    190p., photos, maps, appendices, name lists, index.
    ISBN: 0-912526-55-6: $32.50 trade
    1. Roswell (Ga.) — History. 2. United States — History — Civil War,
1861-1865 — Collaborationists. 3. Treason — History — Civil War, 1861-
1865 — Collaborationists. I. Title.
F294, R75H583   1992
973.7'37   91-36379
                                                              LC

Dedication

To my wife Mary Ann for the many hours over the years that she took care of the family while I was researching another clue or writing the manuscript: and for her typing skills of which I have none. Without her, I could not have written this book.

Table of Contents

List of Maps and Illustrations

—Maps—

—Illustrations—

Preface

This book is about the town of Roswell, Georgia, located 20 miles north of Atlanta and the fate of 400 mill workers during the American Civil War. General W.T. Sherman, in May of 1864, launched a campaign to capture Atlanta. By July of that year, his left flank was in Roswell and this event has raised questions for over 100 years—What really happened in Roswell? What became of the 400 men, women, and children that were charged with treason? In this book the facts are put before the reader, as detailed as possible, for the author believes this is as close as one can get to a historical event without going back into time.

Michael D. Hitt
March, 1991
Georgia

Acknowledgments

My sincere appreciation for assistance goes to the following:

Mary Ann, my wife, for assisting in my research and preparation of the manuscript.
Jerry L. Hitt, my father.
Brad Pruden, Marietta, Ga.
Chuck Brown, Norcross, Ga.
Dennis Kelly, National Park Service, Marietta, Ga.
Julie Negley, Macon, Ga.
Mmes. Katharine Baker Simpson and **Lois Simpson**, Roswell, Ga.
Monroe M. King, Douglasville, Ga.
Glenn W. Sunderland, Washington, Ill.
Eddie Roberts, Atlanta, Ga.
Mr. and Mrs. W. Johnson, Hinsdale, Ill.
Dr. David Evans, Athens, Ga.
Wayne Shelly, Rome, Ga.
George H. Kendley, Marietta, Ga.
Charles B. Castner, CSX Rail Transport Group, Louisville, Ky.
Atlanta City Library
Georgia Institute of Technology Library
University of Georgia Library

Decatur City Library, Decatur, Ga.
Lake Lanier Regional Library System,
Gwinnett Co., Ga.
Indiana State Library
Pennsylvania State Library
New York State Library
Kennesaw National Battlefield Park Library, Marietta, Ga.
Chickamauga National Military Battlefield Park Library,
Chickamauga, Ga.
Library of Congress, Washington, D.C.
Chicago Historical Society Research Library
Syracuse University Library, Syracuse, N.Y.
Tennessce State Library and Archives, Nashville, Tn.
Louisville Public Library, Louisville, Ky.
Georgia Department of Archives and History,
Atlanta, Ga.
National Archives, Washington, D.C.
Alabama Department of Archives and History,
Montgomery, Al.
Filson Club, Louisville, Ky.
Atlanta Magazine, Atlanta, Ga.
Chattahoochee River National Recreation Area Hdqtrs.
Marietta National Cemetery Archives, Marietta, Ga.

Michael D. Hitt
March, 1991
Georgia

Prologue

Roswell, Georgia was founded by Roswell King, who moved from Darien, Georgia, and with his son Barrington, built a cotton mill on the banks of Vickery's Creek in 1839. The cotton mill was known as the Roswell Manufacturing Company and became the largest cotton mill in North Georgia when the company expanded in 1854. At the onset of the American Civil War, the mill town had four mills operating on Vickery's Creek, which empties into the Chattahoochee River. The Ivy Woolen Mill, owned by Roswell King's grandsons, James and Thomas King, was located at the mouth of Vickery's Creek. The two Roswell cotton mills, owned by Barrington King, were located 3/4 of a mile north of the Ivy mill. The Lebanon flour mill, owned by the Roswell Manufacturing Company, was located 1 1/2 mile north of the last cotton mill. These mills were important to the Confederate Government for the material they produced. They were equally important to the people that lived in Roswell because the mills were their means of support for their families. By July 6, 1864, all this would change.

The Confederate unit guarding Roswell, was named the Roswell Battalion, organized on June 28, 1863. According to 1863 and 1864 Confederate Military Records:

This company was formed of men transferred from Captain Thomas E. King's Company which was divided and formed Companies A, B, and C, Roswell Battalion Georgia Volunteers. This company is organized for home defense to protect the portion of the State of Georgia lying north of Atlanta to the Alabama and Tennessee lines (under the act of Congress for home defense), not to be called upon except to repel a raid of the Yankees and not to be kept on service longer than is necessary for that special purpose. A large portion are composed of detailed men not at work for C. State Government under Major G.W. Cunningham, Q.M. for Atlanta at Roswell Factories, 20 miles north of Atlanta. It is composed of men and boys from 60 years down to 16 years of age. This company was originally a battalion of Infantry, Cavalry and Artillery, organized for local defense and composed principally of men detailed to operate the cotton and woolen mills at Roswell, Cobb Co., Georgia having been ordered by our forces, a number of the men deserted; after which the Captain comd' g the battalion was ordered to turn over the artillery and mount the remainder of the men, they mounting themselves.[1]

Roster of the Roswell Battalion

Adams, Lt Theodore D.
Albritten, Pvt James L.
Allen, Pvt Martin
Allgood, Pvt Nathan
Anderson, Pvt J.M.
Arnold, Pvt John W.
Ashley, Pvt John
Bailey, Pvt John
Ball, Sgt M.
Barker, Pvt James
Barker, Pvt John
Bentley, Pvt William A.
Bolton, Pvt W.H.
Bonfoy, Pvt Samuel
Bownlee, Pvt B.W.
Boyce, Pvt M.
Boyles, Pvt William R.
Bradford, Pvt James
Brown, Pvt A.P.
Brown, Pvt B.W.
Brown, Pvt H.
Brown, Pvt John C.
Brown, Sgt John J.
Brown, Sgt John N.
Brown, Pvt Melvin P.
Brown, Ord Sgt Cisero S.
Bryant, Pvt A.F.
Bryant, Pvt P.H.
Burnett, Pvt John
Bush, Sgt Asa
Cain, Pvt H.
Camp, Pvt E.J.
Camp, Pvt George H.
Cassells, Pvt Thomas
Cassells, Pvt William
Clark, Capt J.P.
Cobb, Pvt D.D.
Cobb, Pvt Durand
Cobb, Pvt James
Cobb, Pvt James Thompson
Coleman, Pvt E.
Coleman, Pvt John
Coleman, Pvt William

Cooley, Pvt George F.
Cooley, Pvt John
Copeland, Pvt Andrew J.
Couch, Pvt A.N.
Cronan, Pvt Joseph
Cruse, Pvt S.O.
Dodgen, Sgt Wiley
Dodgen, Pvt, William R.
Drake, Pvt John
Dremon, Pvt J.W.
Dunwody, Capt Charles A.
Dupree, Corp Benjamin H.
Eades, Corp George W..
Echols, Pvt P.
Ellenbury, Pvt J.E.
Elliott, Pvt John L.
Farr, Pvt Johnathan
Faulkner, Sgt C.W.
Fenn, Pvt T.A.
Fields, Pvt J.F.
Fields, Sgt P.C.
Flowers, 2Lt B.J.
Fortner, Sgt Charles W.
Fretwell, Pvt Isaac
Fretwell, Pvt Littleton B.
Gaddy, Corp P.S.
Gann, Pvt George
Garrett, Pvt William
Garrison, Pvt John
Garrison, Pvt P.
Garrison, Pvt T.W.
Gilbert, Sgt William
Green, Pvt H.M.
Green, Pvt Newton
Grey, Pvt Andrew W.
Grimes, Pvt John
Groover, Pvt Milton
Groover, Pvt Peter
Groover, Sgt Raford J.
Groover, Sgt Raybond J.
Hindman, Pvt Asel
Hopkins, Pvt George W.
Hopkins, Pvt W.C.

Hunter, Pvt James S.
Hunter, Pvt J.J.
Jackson, Pvt J.E.
Jackson, Sgt(Farrier) Lewis A.
Jenkins, Pvt J.W.
Jones, Pvt B.W.
Jones, Pvt Singleton
Kelly, Pvt James
Kelpin, Pvt Charles
King, Capt James R.
King, 1Lt Joseph H.
King, Sr. 1Lt Ralph B.
King, Capt Thomas E.
Kinley, Pvt Hugh
Kinley, 3Lt John R.
Kirk, Pvt Frank
Kirk, Corp Henry
Lamb, Pvt E.S.
Lewis, Pvt James
Lindsey, Corp Ransom
Long, Pvt Reuben
Low, Pvt Samuel
Mackey, Pvt Harris
Mackey, Pvt Simon
Manwaring, Sgt J.
Mayfield, Corp H.
McGullion, Pvt Albert J.
McGullion, Corp Matthew R.
Medlin, Pvt George
Medlin, Corp Joel J.
Medlin, Pvt John
Medlin, Corp R.J.
Minhinnett, 2Lt Frank J.
Minhinnett, Pvt John
Mitchell, Pvt Jessee
Moon, Pvt John
Moore, Pvt John
Newman, Pvt William
Nix, Pvt William
Norris, Pvt James
Osborn, Pvt B.W.
Owens, Pvt David
Owens, Pvt William
Paden, Pvt Robert S.
Poore, Pvt Gresham
Pratt, Jr. 1Lt Charles
Pratt, Pvt William
Pryor, 1Lt James J.

Quinn, Pvt Thomas
Reddings, Pvt Kinson
Reeves, Pvt Benjamin
Reynolds, Pvt J.T.
Ridens, Pvt Kinson
Riding, Pvt K.
Roberts, Pvt J.H.
Roberts, Sgt John
Roberts, Pvt John W.
Roberts, Pvt William S.
Robinson, Corp John
Roche, Pvt Theodore
Sherman, Pvt John
Sherman, Pvt Luther
Sherman, Pvt Nat
Sherman, 2Lt Randolph E.
Sigman, Pvt E.
Smith, Pvt E.W.
Smith, Pvt Henry
Smith, Pvt John
Smith, Sgt S.D.
Sprayberry, Pvt B.
Steadley, Pvt D.B.
Stephens, Pvt Thomas S.
Steward, Pvt James A.
Swords, Pvt John
Thompson, Pvt James H.
Torbush, Pvt James
Touchstone, 2Lt Soloman
Voss, Sgt Nat
Waldrop, Corp Harry
Wallace, Pvt Amanias
Watkins, Sr. 2Lt Gary
Watson, Pvt Benjamin W.
Watson, Pvt John
Webb, Pvt Clinton M.
West, Sgt Isaac C.
West, Pvt J.T.
Whelchel, Pvt Daniel D.
Whelchel, Pvt Hiram
Whelchel, Pvt Major
Whittington, Sgt J.N.
William, Pvt Jessee
Wing, Pvt John L.
Wood, Pvt Jason S.
Wood, Pvt John
Wood, Pvt William
Zachry, Capt A.A.

James Roswell King
Son of Barrington King
Courtesy of Catherine Simpson

May 1864

Thursday, May 19

On May 19, 1864, Confederate Adjutant A.W. Harris, wrote Capt. James King warning him of a possible raid to Roswell.

Atlanta, Ga. May 19, 1864

Capt. J.R. KING,
Commanding, &c., Roswell, Ga.:
Captain: I am directed by Colonel Wright to say that in view of the activity of the enemy in our front, he desires that the greatest vigilance be exercised by you to prevent surprise &c., at Roswell. He desires that particular care be taken of the artillery in your hands, and that under no circumstances should it fall into the hands of the enemy. No apprehension of trouble is felt from other than raiding parties (cavalry), and they would not, likely, bring artillery with them, and should they get possession of yours, it would enable them greatly to damage us here. He desires that all resistance that can, be offered against the enemy should they attack, and in case they should come in too large force to resist that you fall back this side the river and burn the bridge. He desires that at no time should you lose sight of the imprecaution be taken to prevent it. You will please advise him promptly of any advance of the enemy in your vicinity.

I am, &c.,
A.W. HARRIS
Adjutant.2

1

Barrington King
1798-1866
Courtesy of Roswell Presbyterian Church, History Room

Monday, May 30

Barrington King, upon receiving information of a possible raid to his town, left for Atlanta with members of his family. On May 30, 1864, he wrote the following, to a friend.

Revd W.E. BAKER

Staunton my dear Wm I sent you a few days since wudispatch. So soon as Genl Johnson crossed the Etowah - Mother, Harris, Florrie & myself came to this place, stopping with Mr. Pease. I brought over somethings with the R.M. Co (Roswell Manufacturing Co) books & papers, apprehending a visit from the vandals - we found it impossible to remove the machinery. I concluded to keep the factory in motion to the last hour, sending off yarn etc. as fast as produced. Mr. Eldridge will remain there, Mr. Camp & Ralph as long as practicible - the hands all at work, having divided 2 months provisions with them, it being safer with the people than our store in case of a raid, or capture, should that army approach. If the vandals are west of the R.R. we may escape, but very great danger - it is sad to be forced from a comfortable home, but our trust is in God for direction....

B. KING.3

Meanwhile, Capt. James King, Barrington King's son, was preparing his woolen mill for the coming raid. Four years after the war, James King wrote the following statement for the Superior Court of Fulton Co., State of Georgia.

I left the mill in charge of my head man & told them (& the Hands) to remain at their post or in their houses until driven out & to protect the property if they could....4

General W.W. Mackall
(C.S.A.)
Generals In Gray, 1959

June 1864

Sunday, June 12

By June, General Sherman's union army was only 14 miles west of Roswell, at Kennesaw mountain. Confederate Chief of Staff W.W. Mackall writes General G.W. Smith, in charge of State troops, to be prepared for a possible raid toward Roswell.

In the Field, June 12, 1864

General G.W. SMITH,
Commanding Georgia State Troops:

General Johnston informs you that the enemy are pushing parties down on our right and threatening raids beyond the Chattahoochee, and he therefore wishes you to use your entire force in watching and guarding the passages of the river as high up as Roswell Factory. He also requests a report of your strength and position when your arrangements are made.

Yesterday I sent you an order to burn the bridge near Roswell Factory; having ascertained that there was a guard of our troops at the bridge the general no longer insists on its immediate destruction, but that arrangements be made so that it can be destroyed when it can no longer be defended.

I am, sir very respectfully, your obedient servant,

W.W. MACKALL
Chief of Staff.

P.S. There is a shallowford half mile below the bridge on the Marietta road, not guarded. Colonel Lee is reported to have a force of 400 to 500 men and four pieces of artillery at the bridge.

W.W. MACKALL
Chief of Staff.5

**General William T. Sherman
(U.S.)**
National Archives

6

July 1864

Friday, July 1

The 400 to 500 troops at Roswell withdrawn and sent 20 miles down river to support the Confederate Left Flank. Only the Roswell Battalion remains.

Sunday, July 3

General Johnston, in command of the Confederate troops in Georgia, withdraws his army from the Kennesaw line and retreats, south, through Marietta. The Roswell Battalion and the citizens of Roswell are preparing for the expected raid. Captain W.H. Clark of the battalion writes the following note to Ralph King.

Dear RALPH,

A report having reached me that Marietta was evacuated last night, I sent this request that you will come over immediately to hold a consultation in regard to what is best to be done.

I would advise the ladies to be in readiness to leave immediately and Mrs. Tom King* with her children especially. Come over as soon as possible, Capt. Echols and others await your arrival.

Captain WILL H. CLARK
Commander, Roswell Battalion
and Post.6

[*Mrs. Tom King is Mary Read Clemens, wife of Capt. Thomas Edward King. Mrs. King was living at Bulloch Hall during the Civil War.]

Monday, July 4

General W.T. Sherman orders the 2nd U.S. Cavalry Division to Roswell.

HDQRS. Military Division of the Mississippi,
In the Field, July 4, 1864

General GARRARD,
Commanding Division of Cavalry:

General: I am satisfied the enemy will attempt with his cavalry to cross the Chattahoochee about Roswell and make an attempt on our communications. To counteract him you will move in that direction and watch close, taking some position on which to rally on infantry, a brigade of which is at Marietta, a strong brigade at Allatoona, and General Thomas, will be instructed to hold McCook's brigade ready to go to your assistance. You may draw out at once and go to Roswell, and if you can force your way to it, you may gain a secure position from which you can watch that point. In case the enemy's cavalry get across, you must hang to him, opposing him whenever opposition is possible, and send couriers rapidly to me, and to the points of the railroad threatened. In the mean time report to me frequently and use your cavalry as though you were preparing to cross yourself or were only waiting for the waters to subside and make the ford practicable. You now understand the geography so well that I have no doubt you can prevent Wheeler from doing much damage between Marietta and Allatoona. In case he passes round by Canton to go toward Cartersville, send notice and hang on his rear. We now have a full division of infantry at Kingston. Arrest every citizen in the country whom you find likely to prove a spy, and keep moving so that your force cannot be computed.

I am, & c.,
W.T. SHERMAN,
Major-General, Commanding.7

Brigadier General Kenner Garrard
Second Division Cavalry Commander (U.S.)
Generals in Blue, 1959

Tuesday, July 5

Garrard's mounted division was relieved early this morning, from its lines at Smyrna, Georgia, and marched back north toward Marietta. When within two miles south of Marietta, the column turned east onto the Roswell Road [present day GA 120].

The day was reported to be very hot and very trying on the Federal soldiers.

The First Brigade of Garrard's Second Cavalry Division rode in advance of the other two brigades. From the First Brigade, the Seventh Pennsylvania Cavalry rode in advance. The Seventh found the bridge across Sope Creek in poor condition, but passablc [GA 120 near Providence Road]. It was here, on the east side of the creek, Col. Abram O. Miller camped the Third Brigade of Mounted Infantry for the next three days. Sgt. Benjamin Mager of the Seventy-Second Indiana writes:

Here we had three days' rest, and never more needed, or more enjoyed. The dense shade shielded the burning rays of the sun from our heads, and the woods were so full of blackberries...such large and nice ones...that a man in a few minutes could pick as many as he would want to eat through the day. They were so conducive to health we almost lived upon them. Our custom was to pick for a mess of eight a gallon of blackberries, cover with a gallon of water and bring to a boil, and then stir in three pounds of broken crackers and a pound of sugar, and the gods never ate a better dish.8

The 17th Indiana Mounted Infantry and the 1st Ohio Vol. Cavalry rode a mile and a half south to the paper mill on Sope Creek. After skirmishing with the Roswell Battalion, the mill was burned. The Roswell Battalion fell back toward Roswell with the 9th Tennessee Cavalry (C.S.A.). Pvt. Stephen A. Jordan of the 9th Tennessee Cavalry writes:

...went 2 miles further & dismounted, and a skirmish. We fell back & crossed Chattahoochee River & skirmished across river.9

(The first skirmish occurred in the modern location of GA 120 and Timber Ridge Road.) The First and Second Brigades rode on and camped on the banks of Willeyo Creek. [The First Brigade camped

10

north of the intersection of GA 120 & Willeyo Creek and on the Cobb Co. side. The Second Brigade, with Garrard's headquarters, camped south of GA 120 and 1/2 mile west of the water treatment plant.]

Back in Roswell, 2 miles away, Capt. James King gave instruction to his woolen mill Superintendent, Samuel Bonfoy,

to run the machinery until driven out by the soldiers.10

Then, at 11:00 a.m., the Confederate Battalion from Roswell, numbering 75 mounted men, rode south out of town. After crossing the covered bridge at the Chattahoochee River, Capt. King had the bridge burned, then continued south. [The covered bridge was 30 feet west of the modern bridge, Roswell Road at the river.] The Seventh Pennsylvania Cavalry, Garrard's advance guard, rode along the "River Road" [modern Azalea Road] and reached the bridge too late to save it, but did find at that location the Ivy Woolen Mill [mill site - in small patch of woods east of north end of river bridge.] News of the Seventh's arrival was sent to Garrard who, in turn, wrote a message to Sherman's headquarters.

Captain DAYTON,
Acting Assistant Adjutant General:

Captain: I have to report for the information of the Major- General commanding, that my command is camped on Willeyo Creek near Roswell Factory. My advance is at the factory. I will destroy all buildings. The bridge at this point over the river is burnt by the rebels. The ford [Shallowford] is passable; so reported by citizens. I sent a regiment to the paper mills, burnt the paper mills, flouring mills and machine shops. The citizens report the banks of the river high at Power's Ferry and batteries in position on the south bank. They had a pontoon bridge at Pace's Ferry, a few miles below, where a portion of their army crossed. There is a road running from Roswell Factory down the river below the paper mills, and near the mills and above passes on the bank of the river. As fast as possible I will send in information on the roads, forks, ferries, &c.

Very respectfully, your obedient servant,

K. GARRARD
Brigadier-General,
Commanding Division.11

11

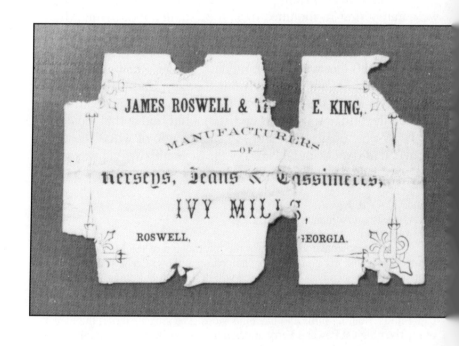

Pre 1865 Business Card of Ivy Woolen Mill

The Roswell Woolen Mill after being rebuilt in 1873.
Courtesy of The Atlanta Historical Society

Meanwhile, back with the advance guard at Roswell Factory, Captain Joseph G. Vale, of company M, Seventh Pennsylvania Cavalry writes:

The proprietors of the mills, soon after our entry onto the place, called upon our officers, and declaring they were subjects of Great Britain and of France under the protection of these nations, demanded that the rights of neutrals be respected in themselves, and their property. They were assured that if in fact neutrals, and not found to be, or having been engaged in aiding the Southern belligerants, the rights claimed would be fully accorded and respected. Meanwhile, the work in the mills went on regularly, as though no hostile forces were present.[12]

Wednesday, July 6

The men from the three mounted brigades spent a good bit of their time gathering food for their horses and themselves. John A. Nourse of the Chicago Board of Trade Battery writes:

Today the horses stand still, but the men are all over the country picking berries, cherries and apples, and getting wheat for the horses. The rest is very much needed.[13]

Garrard himself made a visit to the Roswell Mill [Woolen Mill], to check on the citizens' claims of neutrality as were made to Capt. Vale. Captain writes:

...some officers, we are not allowed to name, but are of the opinion that General Gerrard (sic) was the ranking one, stepped into the factory and passing through, found the operators busy engaged in making heavy cotton cloth, and a very little investigation showed that on each Webb, of piece, the cabalistic letters, C.S.A., were woven in the wool. The 'neutral subjects of Great Britain' and 'Imperial France' were sent for, their attention called to these facts, and they were told to take down the French Flag, which was flying at the flagstaff, remove their money and private papers, subject to proper supervision, and notify all the operators to leave the building at once. On their refusal to do so, a guard was called in and soon cleared the building. All the books and papers, &c., of the company were seized, placed under guard, and duly forwarded to army headquarters. When this preliminary work had been done, the buildings were fired in many places, and with their contents, machinery and stock on hand, thoroughly destroyed.[14]

14

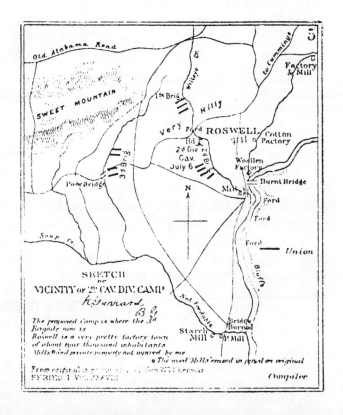

**Sketch of Roswell, Ga., July 5, 1864, sent to
U.S. Headquarters by Brig. Gen Kenner Garrard.**
The Official Military Atlas of the Civil War

Besides the French flag flying over the woolen mill, another was being flown at Bulloch Hall, Capt. Thomas King's widow's residence. Capt. Darius E. Livermore of the 3rd Ohio Cavalry took both flags and gave the owner, Theophile Roche, a receipt for the property:

> Provost Marshall Hd. Qrs.
> Roswell, GA July 6, 1864
>
> This will certify that the bearer Mr. Theophile Roche has voluntarily given the undersigned two French flags. His property will receive the same protection as though the flags still remained on this premises.
> D.E. LIVERMORE
> Capt. 3rd Post Commander[15]

[In 1882, Roswell's Postmaster, Theodore D. Adams, wrote a statement used in the French and American Claims commission that a French flag flew over widow Thomas E. King's home, when the Federal troops came to Roswell.]

While inspection of the other mills started, Garrard sent a message to Sherman stating that he had taken possession of Roswell. Sherman, in turn, sent a reply:

> Hdqrts. Military Division of the
> Mississippi. In the Field, near
> Chattahoochee, July 6, 1864
>
> General GARRARD:
>
> General: - I have just received your note announcing that you have possession of Roswell, This is important; watch well the crossing there, but not in force; keep your main force concealed somewhat. General McCook has just started for some point between Rottenwood, and Soap [Sope] Creek, where he will be near you. I propose to throw Schofield over on that flank the moment I propose to attempt a crossing; fords are much better than bridges, and therefore have the river examined well as to fords. I am on the main road at the point where a branch goes to Vining's on the railroad. Howard is at Vining's and has possession at Pace's. McPherson's right is at Howell's Ferry, below Nickajack. The enemy holds this bank from the railroad bridge down to Nickajack, and seems to have it well fortified. Atlanta is in plain view. Stoneman threatens the river down to Sweetwater. I will soon have a telegraph

to Vining's and you can then communicate by Marietta. You will have rest for a few days and should take advantage of all grain fields.

Yours Truly,
W.T. SHERMAN
Major-General, Commanding.16

Col. Abram O. Miller of the Seventy-Second Indiana Mounted Infantry, with a detail of men, went to the cotton mills to destroy them. Before this deed was started, cotton cloth was taken out to be used in the Federal Hospitals. After that, John A. Nourse writes:

The Col. gave out all the cloth and the provisions to the girls that were employed there. Fifteen buildings were burnt—one building alone employed eight hundred girls. There are three mill down, with power enough to give motion to the machinery of six such mills as the Bay State Mills of Mass.17

[The large cotton mill is located 400 feet south of Founder's Cemetery on Sloan Street, down on Vickery's Creek. The smaller cotton mill site is located about 2/10 of a mile south of the larger cotton mill. The other mill is the woolen mill.]

Pvt Silas C. Stevens, of the Chicago Board of Trade Battery, was also in this detail. He wrote the following of his involvement at the cotton mills.

On our arrival these mills were in full running capacity. The aide asked the proprietor to be shown around the works, to see the working of the machinery. The work that was turned out, and the number of women, girls, and children employed. In fact, everything connected with the manufacture of rebel goods, and capacity of the entire factory.

After all these items of interest were shown us, with the greatest politeness, and civilty on the part of the aide, McCloud, he informed the proprietor or manager, of General Sherman's instructions, and requested the man to stop the machinery, and have all the employees out of the building quickly, that he was ordered to burn the place.

The entire machinery running to its full capacity when we entered the building this order, and information given, came suddenly to a full stop.

The women and children filed out of the structure at once and stood in quiet wonder on the banks of the stream, watching our preparations for the destruction of the mills. It did seem at first blush, to be a wanton act, to fire those polished machines which filled the building from basement to the top story, after they came to a stand still, but all is fair, it has been stated, in love and war.

The store house nearby was given to me, with two men to assist with orders to fire the structure. The main factory, which was running when we arrived at the place, McCloud reserved for his own hand.

I caused to be placed on each floor, beginning at the top, saturated cotton with oil, in great quantities, and carefully arranged everything ready to fire my building, and waited with courtesy. I did not wait long. I lighted the combustibles which went off with a flash, at the upper story first, then each successive floor, from the top downward to the basement, so that I had a very interesting blaze, at once, while McCloud fired his machinery hall, from the basement, or engine room; by this act the fire of the factory burned more slowly, yet surely.

My idea was not to endanger the buildings of the residents of the place, whose houses were in the immediate vicinity, and if my fire was communicated by floors, from the top downward there would possibly be less danger from flying sparks, and each floor would fall quickly as burned, into the basement and the waters of the stream.

The walls which were very stout would probably remain standing but the contents of the entire edifice would be consumed.

These orders which were strictly carried out, and my structure was under way very quickly and was a complete success; and long before the factory was well started the contents of my building were entirely consumed. I took a great deal of pleasure in helping burn these factories, and from this time on, till the end of the war, orders of this kind, I greatly enjoyed, and many a bale of cotton and gin mills of every description my hand fired...

Before the completion of the burning of my building, and beyond a rescue from destruction, McCloud gave me permission, accompanied by one man, to return to camp and report of the success of the undertaking...

My return to camp was easily accomplished in safety and the report made of the success of the destruction of the factories, now apart of history and the progress of the war.[18]

After Garrard finished inspecting the Roswell area and the destruction to the mills, he sent a report to General Sherman informing him of what he found.

Manufacturing Company after being destroyed by fire.
Sketch made by Pvt. Charles Holyland of the
Chicago Board of Trade Battery.
Courtesy of Charlie Salter

Headquarters Cavalry Division
Near Roswell, July 6, 1864 - 7 p.m.

Major General SHERMAN,
Commanding Army:

General: Roswell was occupied by my command with but small opposition, the few hundred rebels on the roads falling back before my advance, and burned the bridge after crossing. There is a good ford at this place, so I am informed [the shallowford], but as the opposite banks command this one, and pickets lie on the other side, I have not crossed any of my men. The approach to Roswell from Marietta can be made on two roads—one, as it approaches within miles of Roswell, is by a crooked, hilly road that could be easily defended; the other, river road, passes so close to the river as to come under fire of the enemy's rifles. I had one man shot of this road from the other side. There are branch roads which lead into Cummings road and the Old Alabama road, and the approach on the latter is the best and safest in case the enemy is in this vicinity or secrecy is desirable. The position in the rear of Roswell for me is not good, as roads come in all directions, but by being on Soap Creek I can watch all this country, the fords, &c., and passing west of Sweat Mountain will have the short line of the enemy. There is a road leading over to the Old Alabama road a distance of about two miles. As fast as I can gain information I will send it to you.

My impression is that Johnston will make no attempt on this flank, but that his cavalry has gone to his left. He will try to keep his communications with the source of his supplies westward. All information from Citizens and his acts in this vicinity lead to this belief. His cavalry instead of falling back to the fords and bridges in this locality crossed on the bridges, &c., with the Infantry. Everything is taken out of this country; the grain cut by the rebel soldiers and hauled off. All citizens of property also left. There were some fine factories here, an woolen factory, capacity 30,000 yards a month, and has furnished up to within a few weeks 15,000 yards per month to the rebel government, the Government furnished men and material. Capacity of cotton factory 216 looms, 191,086 yards per month, and 51,666 pounds of thread, and 4,229 pounds of cotton rope. This was worked exclusively for the rebel government. The other cotton factory, one mile and a half from town, I have no data concerning. There was six month's supply of cotton on hand. Over the woolen factory the french flag was flying, but seeing no federal flag above it I had the Building burnt. All are burnt. The cotton factory was worked up to the time of its destruction, some 400 women being employed. There was some cloth which I will save for our hospitals [several thousand yards of cotton cloth], also some rope and thread. I just learned that McCook is near the paper-mills, on Soap Creek, and I may not take up position first proposed in this letter, I will try to disguise the strength of my command. The machinery of the cotton factory cost before the war $400,000. The superintendent estimates that it alone was worth with its material, &c., when burnt over a million of our money.

Very respectfully, your obedient servant,

K. GARRARD
Brigadier-General Commanding.19

John A. Nourse, of the Chicago Board of Trade Battery, commented on these mills and their owners.

These mills and the whole country around here is owned by the King & Co. They own all the stores, provisions etc; they allow no liquor sold in town, and in truth run everything to suit themselves—Had their own paper currency, which circulated all through this country as better than Confederate scrip—the Kings left town with their "hard money" in a wagon the night before we came in—the niggers say a wagon full—yellow money in chests—the town had one thousand inhabitants besides the factory girls.20

Lieutenants Worley and Allen, of Signal Detachment, Seventeenth Army Corps, reported to General Garrard on Roswell. General Sherman ordered the two officers to that location to set a signal station, so he could send and receive messages much quicker than by courier. Signal stations were also set up on Black-Jack Mountain, Kennesaw Mountain, and at General Sherman's Headquarters in Vinings.

The 9th Tennessee Cavalry (C.S.A.), who had been on the south shore of the Chattahoochee River, at Roswell, rode east to guard McAfee's Bridge. [McAfee's Bridge was then the next covered bridge upstream from the Roswell Bridge.]

Thursday, July 7

After Garrard's report the night before, General Sherman sent back a reply:

Hdqrs. Military Division of the
Mississippi. In the field, near
Chattahoochee, July 7, 1864

General GARRARD:

General: Your report is received and is most acceptable. I had no idea that the factories at Roswell remained in operation, but supposed the machinery had all been removed. Their utter destruction is right and meets my entire approval, and to make the matter complete you will arrest the owners and employees and send them, under guard, charged with treason to Marietta, and I will see as to any man in America hoisting the French flag and then devoting his labor and capital in supplying armies in open hostility to our Government and claiming the benefit of his neutral flag. Should you, under the impulse of anger, natural at contemplating such perfidy, hang the wretch, I approve the act beforehand. I have sent General Schofield to reconnoiter over on that flank, and I want a Lodgement made on the other banks as soon as possible anywhere from Roswell down to the vicinity of Soap Creek. I have no doubt the opposite bank is picketed, but, as you say, the main cavalry force of Wheeler has moved to the other flank an we should take advantage of it. If you can make a Lodgement on the south bank anywhere and secure it well, do so. General Schofield will be near to follow it up and enlarge the foothold. He has just started from Ruff's station a few minutes before I received your dispatch, but I telegraphed the substance to be sent to overtake him. Keep a line of couriers back to Marietta and telegraph me fully and often. I now have the wires to my bivouac. By selecting some one ford, say the second or third below the mouth of Willeyo Creek, on your sketch, and holding a force there concealed, say a brigade with your battery, then have the heads of each of your other two brigades close by above and below at the nearest fords, let detachments from these latter brigades cross at night at the nearest fords, and without firing a gun, close in front of the brigade in position to cross with Artillery. When across with Artillery the best position on a commanding hill should be fortified. I will see that the cavalry is relieved by General Schofield at once. I merely suggest this plan and its execution about daylight tommorrow, and I prefer you should do it.

I assure you, spite of any little disappointment I may have expressed, I feel for you personally not only respect but affection, and wish for your unmeasured success and reputation, but I do wish to inspire all cavalry with my conviction that caution and prudence should be but a small element in their characters.

I repeat my orders that you arrest all people, male and female, connected with those factories, no matter what the clamor, and let them foot it, under guard, to Marietta, whence I will send them by cars to the North. Destroy and make some disposition of all mills save small flouring mills manifestly for local use, but all sawmills, and factories dispose of effectually, and useful laborers excused by reason of the skill as manufacturers from conscription, are as much prisoners as if armed. The poor women will make a howl. Let them take along their children and clothing, provided they have the means of hauling or you can spare them. We will retain them until they can reach a country where they can live in peace and security.

In your next letter give me as much information as you can as to the size and dimensions of the burned bridge at Roswell across the Chattahoochee. We have plenty of Pontoon bridging, but I much prefer fords for so large an army as we have.

I am, with respect, yours truely,

W.T. SHERMAN
Major-General, Commanding.[21]

All through the day, mounted patrols rode to the different fords in the Roswell area and then reported back to Garrard of their finds. At 5 p.m. Garrard writes:

…The only good ford I can hear of is at this point. The Island Ford, three miles above, is good for footmen, but no roads lead to it or from it, and on the other side it is thick woods and very hilly and two miles over to the Atlanta road. This ford could be used to secure the lower one, but not for artillery, cavalry, of wagons until we hold the other bank and make a road. I can hear of no practicable fords except these within fifteen miles of this place. McAfee's Bridge is not burnt and the rebels hold it.[22]

[Island Ford is located North of the city limits, on Riverside Road, at the shoals. McAfee's Bridge site is 30 feet down stream from the present location of the intersection of Holcomb Bridge Road and the Chattahoochee River.]

Friday, July 8

The 9th Tennessee Cavalry (C.S.A.) withdraws from McAfee's Bridge and rides to the support of Confederate units in the area of Sope's Creek. This was due to the crossing of elements of the 23rd Army Corps. Sope's Creek enters the Chattahoochee River approximately 3 1/2 miles downstream from the Roswell Bridge.

At Roswell, the mill workers had been gathered and placed under guard in town. Woolen mill Loom Boss, John N. Brown, writes:

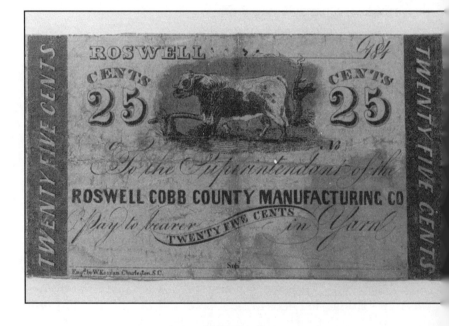

Roswell Currency
(Author's Private Collection)

We all started from Roswell with a wagon train furnished us by the army the evening of the 7th about 7 o'clk going to Marietta.23

While this was taking place, Colonel Miller went down to the Shallowford to get an idea of the area he was going to cross his troops. [The shallowford crossing is at the modern location where the children's playground is, in the Fulton Co. Park. on Azalea Road.] Colonel Miller writes:

Came down to the river today to look at the ford where I am to cross the men of my brigade, under fire of the enemy, whom I can see behind the works on the opposite side of the river.24

Dr. Cole of the Seventy-Second Indiana writes:

By a reconnaissance of the ford a mile from Roswell, today it was found that the rebels were guarding it in force, and as we design crossing it, if possible, early tomorrow morning, at this point, we may have some work to do. Consequently I have taken charge of the Presbyterian church, place the sick in it, and am prepared for the contest.25 [This is the same Presbyterian Church on Mimosa Boulevard.]

While Federal officers were observing the confederates at the ford, the Confederates were keeping a close eye on the Federals. Confederate Lt. Col. J.F. Gaines of Wheeler's Cavalry report.

Burnt Bridge, July 8, 1864

Captain TERRETT
Kelly's Headquarters:
Captain: In accordance with report sent in by Lieutenant Cotton commanding picket, first post above burnt bridge, the enemy is moving with considerable force up the river in the direction of McAfee's Bridge; they have with them four wagons, supposed to be pontoon bridges. They have been quite busy during this afternoon, just opposite us on the river, at work on the timber. Their move commenced about dark.
Very respectfully,
J. F. GAINES
Lieutenant-Colonel, Commanding. 26

Roswell Presbyterian Church
Courtesy of Roswell Presbyterian Church History Room

Shortly after Lt. Col. Gaines sent the last message to headquarters, he sent another, as more of his scouts were reporting in.

Headquarters Hannon's Brigade,
July 8, 1864 - about 5 p.m.

Captain TERRETT,
Assistant Adjutant - General, Kelly's Division:

Captain: Scouting parties of the enemy have made their appearance all along my front to-day as far up as McAfee's Bridge. I think very likely they are reconnoitering for the purpose of attempting a crossing at some point. I have sent another scout across the river on foot, with instructions to go in the rear of the enemy, and advise me of their movements. I am picketing and scouting about five miles above McAfee's Bridge, and have about 200 men on the line below the bridge. I enclose you a dispatch just received from Captain Mastin; having ordered the fords picketed which he describes.

J.F. GAINES
Lieutenant-Colonel.27

As the 53rd Alabama Cavalry watched the Shallowford and the 24th Alabama Battalion watched the area about McAfee's Bridge; Garrard was moving his federal troops into Roswell. At 6:00 p.m. the different sections of the Chicago Board of Trade Battery, having been gathered in one place, marched into Roswell and camped in the center of town. The rest of the division was mounted up and marched to the very western edge of Roswell where they camped. Orders were put out to keep as quiet as possible and not to build any camp fires. It was reported to have been a cool night. The only other military operation on this day near Roswell, was the crossing of portions of the Twenty-third Army Corps of the Army of the Ohio under Major-General Schofield, on the Chattahoochee at the mouth of Sope Creek. This crossing was successful and a complete surprise to the confederate outpost on the Fulton County side.

**Private Wilson Henderson, member of Company A,
98 Illinois Mounted Infantry**
Courtesy of Glenn W. Sunderland

Saturday, July 9

At 2:00 a.m. Federal General John Newton is directed to move his division to Roswell, at 4:30 a.m., and support Garrard;

Making sure of anything that may be gained by him.28

Back in Roswell, at 3:00 a.m. the Fourth Ohio Vol. Cavalry saddled up and rode for McAfee's Bridge. The regiment was ordered to hold the bridge, prevent Confederate troops from crossing or destroying it. The rest of the second brigade saddled their horses and were held as reserves, to be ready to move at the shortest notice. The first and third brigades were also awakened at 3:00 a.m. These two brigades left their horses in town and started marching south on foot. It was reported to be a moonless night. The men of the third brigade started out first. Of this brigade, the Seventeenth Indiana and the Ninety Eighth Illinois marched down the main road leading to the shallowford. [Main road is present day Chattahoochee Street.] The Seventy-Second Indiana and the One Hundred Twenty-Third Illinois took a road to the left so as to strike the river about 200 yards above the main road. [This road to the left is the present day South Atlanta Street.] The closer the men got to the river, the foggier it got, which entirely concealed their movements. Two companies of the Seventeenth Indiana and two companies (D and I) of the Seventy-Second Indiana, were deployed as skirmishers at the river's edge and hidden in the brush. This skirmish line extended 300 yards along the bank of the river. Colonel Miller writes:

At the same time one company from the Seventy-Second and two from the Seventeenth were deployed as sharpshooters on the bluffs on this side, to engage the attention of the enemy and protect my skirmishers while crossing.29

John Nourse of the Chicago Board of Trade Battery writes:

...After breakfast the first four guns went with Lieut.'s R. and G. and took their positions on the bluff commanding the ford.30

[The battery site is now the cul-de-sac of Spring Drive.] The river was four hundred yards wide, and the fog so heavy upon the water that the men could not see across, and it seemed so deep that scarcely a man dreamed they were expected to cross. Capt. Thomson says he really expected that they should lay a pontoon across the river, never suspecting the real work that was before him. The Captain, on his way to report to Col. MIller, and when halfway up the hill, turned to view the situation. It was then getting a little light, and he could see a big white house on yon side of the river, and a lot of soldiers sleeping on the porch, and the sentinels at regular interval along the line of the river, and others passing up and down the hill in numbers sufficient to convince him that it would be hazardous to undertake to cross, if indeed, they were expected to cross.

The rebels seemed all unconscious of an enemy near them. The Captain reports to Col. Miller, and said his men were deployed and in position. *Well,* said the Colonel, *As soon as the Artillery opens, move your men right across.* The captain for a moment was struck with astonishment, but immediately replied, *You don't mean to say that we are expected to wade that river? Yes, that is what we have been sent here for, and we expect to do it.* The captain says he never realized anything in his life that looked so extremely perilous as that did; *if you order it, we will try it.* Col. Miller says that just at the time he overheard some men in the main line of battle debating the propriety of crossing, when one of the men said: *By G-d, I'll not believe it till Miller says so!* When Capt. Thomson got back to his men, all of them seemed to have been discussing the matter, and the first words he heard were: *We'll never cross it,'* and the next were: *If they ordered us to we'll do it; but I don't believe Col. Miller will order us to.*31

Suddenly the Artillery opened fire. John A. Nourse writes:

Our guns shelled the bluffs across the river, but got no reply. The caissons moved up and remained with the guns.32

Sgt. Mager observed,

...the Artillery belches forth a volley of shells, which burst among the sleeping sentinels with the sound of mighty thunder. Capt. Thomson gives the command *'forward!'* and without a moment's hesitancy the men plunge into the water up to the armpits. Not a faltering one; not a Laggard! But with a cheer they rushed into the water and charged for the other shore. General Garrard now rides to the water's edge and cheers them on shouting, *Bully boys! Bully Boys! Whiskey in the morning!* The whole brigade now rises up, and with cheer after cheer, urges them forward, while the battery men work away at their guns, determined that the expedition shall not fail for want of energy on their part. However, it is not all smooth sailing with our brave men in the water. As the shells burst among the sleeping rebels on the opposite bank, they started up in the wildest fright, and realize for the first time that the Yankees are upon them.

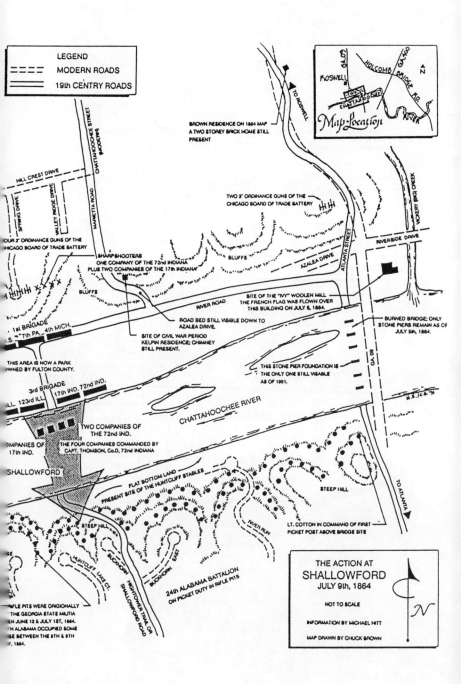

LEGEND
- - - - MODERN ROADS
——— 19th CENTRY ROADS

BROWN RESIDENCE ON 1864 MAP
A TWO STOREY BRICK HOME STILL
PRESENT

TO ROSWELL

ROSWELL RD.
HOLCOMB BRIDGE RD.
CHATTAHOOCHEE
Map Location

HILL CREST DRIVE
SPRING DRIVE
VALLEY RIDGE DRIVE
CHATTAHOOCHEE STREET (MODERN)
MARIETTA ROAD

TWO 3" ORDINANCE GUNS OF THE
CHICAGO BOARD OF TRADE BATTERY

VICKERY (BIG) CREEK

RIVERSIDE DRIVE

OUR 3" ORDINANCE GUNS OF THE
HICAGO BOARD OF TRADE BATTERY

ATLANTA STREET

AZALEA DRIVE

SHARPSHOOTERS
ONE COMPANY OF THE 72nd INDIANA
PLUS TWO COMPANIES OF THE 17th INDIANA

BLUFFS

BLUFFS

RIVER ROAD

SITE OF THE "IVY" WOOLEN MILL
THE FRENCH FLAG WAS FLOWN OVER
THIS BUILDING ON JULY 5, 1864.

BURNED BRIDGE; ONLY
STONE PIERS REMAIN AS OF
JULY 5th, 1864.

1st BRIGADE
S. 7th PA. 4th MICH.

ROAD BED STILL VISIBLE DOWN TO
AZALEA DRIVE.

SITE OF CIVIL WAR PERIOD
KELPIN RESIDENCE; CHIMNEY
STILL PRESENT.

THIS AREA IS NOW A PARK
WNED BY FULTON COUNTY.

THIS STONE PIER FOUNDATION IS
THE ONLY ONE STILL VISABLE
AS OF 1991.

3rd BRIGADE
LL 123rd ILL.
17th IND. 72nd IND.

GA 09

H.R./C.R. 94

CHATTAHOOCHEE RIVER

TWO COMPANIES OF
THE 72nd IND.

OMPANIES OF
17th IND.

THE FOUR COMPANIES COMMANDED BY
CAPT. THOMSON, Co.D, 72nd INDIANA

SHALLOWFORD

TO ATLANTA

FLAT BOTTOM LAND
PRESENT SITE OF THE HUNTCLIFF STABLES

STEEP HILL

STEEP HILL

RIVER RUN

LT. COTTON IN COMMAND OF FIRST
PICKET POST ABOVE BRIDGE SITE

HUNTCLIFF LAKE CT.
BLOCKHORN
HIGHTOWER TRAIL OR
SHALLOWFORD ROAD
BLOCKHORN
EAST

24th ALABAMA BATTALION
ON PICKET DUTY IN RIFLE PITS

IFLE PITS WERE ORIGIONALLY
THE GEORGIA STATE MILITIA
EN JUNE 12 & JULY 1ST, 1864.
H ALABAMA OCCUPIED SOME
SE BETWEEN THE 8TH & 9TH
Y, 1864.

THE ACTION AT
SHALLOWFORD
JULY 9th, 1864

NOT TO SCALE

INFORMATION BY MICHAEL HITT

MAP DRAWN BY CHUCK BROWN

N

31

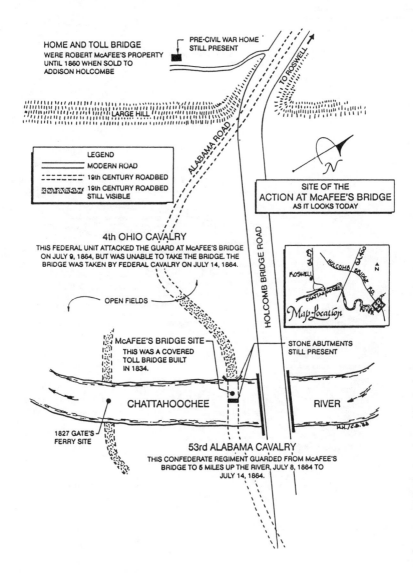

HOME AND TOLL BRIDGE
WERE ROBERT McAFEE'S PROPERTY
UNTIL 1860 WHEN SOLD TO
ADDISON HOLCOMBE

PRE-CIVIL WAR HOME
STILL PRESENT

TO ROSWELL

ALABAMA ROAD

LARGE HILL

LEGEND
MODERN ROAD
19th CENTURY ROADBED
19th CENTURY ROADBED
STILL VISIBLE

N

SITE OF THE
ACTION AT McAFEE'S BRIDGE
AS IT LOOKS TODAY

HOLCOMB BRIDGE ROAD

4th OHIO CAVALRY
THIS FEDERAL UNIT ATTACKED THE GUARD AT McAFEE'S BRIDGE
ON JULY 9, 1864, BUT WAS UNABLE TO TAKE THE BRIDGE. THE
BRIDGE WAS TAKEN BY FEDERAL CAVALRY ON JULY 14, 1864.

OPEN FIELDS

ROSWELL   HOLCOMB BRIDGE RD.
CHATTAHOOCHEE
N
RIVER
Map Location

McAFEE'S BRIDGE SITE
THIS WAS A COVERED
TOLL BRIDGE BUILT
IN 1834.

STONE ABUTMENTS
STILL PRESENT

CHATTAHOOCHEE

RIVER

1827 GATE'S
FERRY SITE

53rd ALABAMA CAVALRY
THIS CONFEDERATE REGIMENT GUARDED FROM McAFEE'S
BRIDGE TO 5 MILES UP THE RIVER, JULY 8, 1864 TO
JULY 14, 1864.

They seize their guns and rush to the water's edge and open upon our men in the river...33

At that moment, writes Colonel Miller
...the enemy opened with a heavy fire, which was vigorously replied to by our sharpshooters from this side, and which attracted their attention from the men in the water.34

According to Captain Vale,
At first the fire was heavy, and the undertaking seemed hazardous, but after getting well into the stream, there about three-fourths of a mile wide, the scene assumed the ludicrous. As before stated, the brigade, in fact, the whole division, was armed with Spencer repeating rifle and carbine, using a metallic waterproof cartridge. The river was very rocky, and in many places the channels between the rocks were found to be 'overhead' in depth. As the rebel bullets began to splash around pretty thick, the boys sought to keep in this deep water with only the head exposed; they soon discovered that they could throw the cartridge from the magazine into the chamber of the piece, by working the lever, as well underwater as in the air; hence, all along the line you could see the men bring their guns up, let the water run from the muzzle a moment, then taking quick aim, fire his piece and pop down again, with only his head exposed. Now, the rebels had never seen anything of this kind before, nor for that matter, had we, and their astonishment knew no bounds.35

By this time, writes Sgt. Mager,
Our men are halfway across the stream, and open fire on the rebels in the brush along the shore. As our men rush up out of the water and immediately open fire with their Spencers, the river is all ablaze, the rebels think that pandemonium has broken loose, and all the imps of the lower regions are now coming for their lawful prey, and they break and run up the hill, our men shooting them in the back. Now there is a race as to who of our brave men shall reach the shore first. The water has gradually become shallower, and now is scarcely to their hips, and such another running, shooting, cheering and splashing, was never witnessed before. Sargt. James A. Mount, Co. D, ever anxious to excel, was perhaps the first to reach the shore, and David Frazier, Co. I, was but little behind him. But where every man of those four companies did his noble, clean best, and each and everyone got there just as quick as he could, we will not be invidious with further distinctions. As our men reach the shore, they rush for the top of the hill and capture three or four prisoners as they ascend, who are blanched and trembling with fright, declaring that our men had just raised up out of the water and commenced to shoot at them. From these prisoners we learned that Martin's whole brigade of cavalry is camped near by as support for the pickets, and we immediately take to the trees, stumps, and logs, for defense. The whole brigade now moves across in column, and

33

our skirmishers are peering into the woods and brush ahead, momentarily expecting Martin's brigade to move upon them, but the frightened fugitives had told the General that Wilder's whole brigade was already across, and he thought discretion was the better part of valor, and contented himself with simply watching our movements. The whole brigade got across in a few minutes, moving out to a good position and went to work throwing up defensive works...36

The first brigade, still on the north bank, was formed up in line of battle and Colonel Minty crossed them immediately. He formed his brigade to the left of the third Brigade. [The Federal troops crossed at the present day location of the Fulton County river park on Azalea Drive and came ashore on the south side of the river where HuntCliff Stables are located.] Then John A. Nourse writes,

The guns of the left section went up the river one half a mile, and into position, but saw no rebels. While we waited for a fight, we got all the potatoes, apples, cucumbers, onions, etc. we could carry.37

Garrard, observing that his men were now in possession of the south ridge, sent a message to General W.T. Sherman at 7:00 a.m., asking for infantry reinforcements. Before Garrard waited for reply, he sent another message at 10:00 a.m.

July 9, 1864 - 10 a.m.
Major-General SHERMAN:
GENERAL: At 7 o'clock I sent you word that I was over the river and had the ridge. I have now a good position, and hold the Roswell and Atlanta road, which passes over the bridge.The ford is a little rough but not deep. All is quiet in my front; but the regiment I sent to take the bridge, eight miles above, failed, and find some considerable force there. They can keep the enemy from burning the bridge, but cannot get possession of it. Prisoners report Kelly's Division, Wheeler's Corps, near that bridge.
Very respectfully, your obedient servant,

K. GARRARD
Brigadier-General.38

Back in town, Dr. Cole stated he had about twenty of the brigade sick at the church. The morning's action claimed no casualties, but some of the sick were probably due to the hot weather.

Chaplain DeLaMatyr, of the Seventy-Second Indiana, preached at the Presbyterian Church around 10:00 a.m. Rev. Pratt was quoted as saying,

...He was not at all pleased with our polluting his house with sick and wounded soldiers. Not withstanding the land of wooden nutmegs was his early home.39

Rev. Pratt was the Roswell preacher for the Presbyterian church. From the diary of the Seventy-Second Indiana it is written;

This morning at 10:00 o'clock the bugle blew for preaching, the first time we had heard it for many a day. Every unemployed soldier about camp went to church, and not withstanding the house was very large, it was well filled. Our whole brigade was composed of men who were in the habit of going to church when at home, and the bugle call for preaching was never unheeded in the army. Our chaplain was universally loved and respected by everyone. The services were unusually impressive, and by contrast with present surroundings brought to mind other scenes far away; and could the common people of the south have been permitted to look upon our devotions, they must have been convinced that we Yankees were not the vandals their leaders had pictured us to be.40

Meanwhile, Brig-General Newton's Division was marching on the Roswell road [present day GA 120] still a few hours away from reaching Roswell. The heat on the soldiers, in their wool uniforms, was taking its toll. Lt. Kyger in Gen Newton's 1st brigade writes:

Twelve M., extremely warm; several sun-strick; two deaths in division from it. Afternoon, we took it more moderate. At 4:45 p.m. came in sight of the Chattahoochie River. Fully two-thirds of division has to straggle; I never have been so hot.41

Captain John Tuttle in Gen. Newton's 3rd Brigade wrote of his experience of the march.

Reverend Nathaniel Pratt
Courtesy of Roswell Presbyterian Church, History Room

The sun was intensely hot and the men suffered greatly. About 11 a.m. we were halted and an Aid came galloping back with orders for me to report to the brigade commander immediately. When I reported, Col. Bradley asked me what those bushes were growing on the side of the road all the way with little burs on them. I told him they were Chinquepins. He said that was all he wanted. I went back to my regiment satisfied that people living north of the Ohio River have very little sense.42

As events on the Federal's left flank were transpiring, attention was given to the Roswell Mill employees as to their future. General Sherman wrote Major-General H.H. Halleck, in Washington, D.C.:

...I call your attention to the enclosed paper in reference to the Roswell Factories. They were very valuable, and were burned by my order. They have been engaged almost exclusively in manufacturing cloth for the Confederate Army, and you will observe they were transferred to the English and French flags for safety, but such nonsense cannot deceive me. They were tainted with treason, and such fictitious transfer was an aggravation. I will send all the owners, agents, and employees up to Indiana to get rid of them there. I take it a neutral is no better than one of our own citizens engaged in supplying a hostile army...43

Then Sherman sent a message to General Webster in Nashville.

Hdqs. Military Division of the
Mississippi, In the field, near
Chattahoochee River, July 9, 1864.

General WEBSTER, Nashville:
I have ordered the arrest of the operators at the Confederate Manufactories at Roswell and Sweet Water, to be sent North. When they reach Nashville have them sent across the Ohio River and turned loose to earn a living where they won't do us any harm. If any of the principals seem to you dangerous, you may order them imprisoned for a time. The men were exempt from conscription by reason of their skill, but the women were simply laborers that must be removed from this district.

W.T. SHERMAN
Major-General, Commanding.44

General Joseph Dana Webster
The Photographic History of the Civil War, 1911

Back at Roswell, elements of General Newton's Division begin to arrive. Captain John Tuttle writes:

We reached Roswell about 4 P.M. and went into bivouac in the vicinity. The men had just time to make a little coffee when we received orders to march two miles further on. Passing through Roswell, waded the Chattahooche and formed in line of battle about a mile beyond. We relieved some cavalry who had some slight fortifications at this place.45

Captain Tuttle also made the following remark on what he observed while passing through Roswell.

About 400 factory girls lined the sides of the road as we passed presenting quite a sad appearance, as they were thrown out of employment and seemed not to know where they would go or what to do.46

Lt. Kyger arrived an hour later, he writes:

Five P.M., we halted near Roswell: got our supper; then we marched through town and down to the river, wading in three different places; 1st brigade farthest up; then one-eighth mile below the 2nd brigade, and about the same distance below it, the 3rd brigade crossed. We took off our pants and socks putting on our shoes again,... Roswell is a small manufacturing village, twelve miles north-east of Marietta. Some nice frame and brick dwellings set back from the streets, in nice shady groves; they look decidedly inviting... There were over eight hundred girls in town; want to go north; a squad of them were sent to Marietta to-day in the supply train. Wilder's brigade dismounted and crossed the river at daylight this morning, not meeting but about sixteen rebs, who seemed to be [posted] for a Lookout; they fled without resistance.47

As the infantry relieved the cavalry on the south shore, the troopers returned to their camps in Roswell. Sgt. Mager wrote:

...we waded back and went into camp where our horses had been all day. The contrast between our feeling on wading back with what they were on going over, was as great as it was agreeable. Many of the men sought to get back to camp with dry clothes by pulling them off and carrying them on top of their heads. Capt. Thomson was among the number, and being a tall man the plan promised success; but he had not reached the middle of the river till he stepped into a luckless hole and fell sprawling in the water, going clear to the bottom, and came near losing his clothes in the bargain. This was more fun than the boys had seen for many a day, and the whole regiment joined in a hearty laugh at the captain's expense.48

125th Ohio Volunteer Infantry. Some of the men of Newton's Division who relieved Garrard's Command.

With the arrival of Newton's Division, Garrard dispatched a report off to General Sherman:

Roswell, July 9, 1864 - 9 P.M.

Major-General SHERMAN:

I have to report the arrival of General Newton with his division, Fourth Corps. All was quiet and he relieved me about dark, My cavalry pickets are about two miles from the river, on the Atlanta road. There has been but slight opposition today, though my cavalry pickets stand opposite to those of the enemy, and have had some skirmishes. No sign of large force of the enemy's infantry. The ford is very rough and about belly deep. Wagons might be passed over though it would be better to have the bridge built. Dimensions of old bridge: Length 642 feet; 6 spans; good stone piers 14 feet from water.

K. GARRARD,
Brigadier-General, Commanding
Cavalry.[49]

By late that night, General Newton's Infantry were finally able to rest. Captain John Tuttle writes:

Weary, worn and wet our men lay down upon the ground about 11 p.m. Owing to the excessive heat of the day very few of us brought our blankets. Had a smart shower of rain during the night. Some little firing just to our right but all was quiet at our front.[50]

Lt. Col. Henry G. Stratton of the 19th Ohio Volunteer Infantry made the following comment after his arrival in Roswell, in a letter home to his sister:

We captured a large factory afire and the operatives eight hundred females, almost enough for one apiece... some were very gay, silks, laces & and were perfectly willing to play the agreeable to the wretched Yankees, others were as cold and rigid as iceburgs...threatening us with all the judgements of Heaven and Southern Confederacy for sins in burning the factory, warehouses and government property thereby stopping the manufacture of 5,000 yards of cloth per day. Awful was'ent it...[51]

Back at McAfee's Bridge the Fourth Ohio Cavalry had been skirmishing all day with the 24th Alabama Cavalry Battalion. Colonel E. Long writes:

Brigadier General John Newton
Fourth U.S. Army Corps
Second Division Commander
The Photographic History of the Civil War, 1911

...the enemy held the farther end of the bridge, and skirmishing with them was continued until evening, when they fell back, and the Fourth Ohio held the bridge entire, having no loss except 1 man wounded. Later in the evening the regiment was ordered back to camp.52

Sunday, July 10

After General Johnston (C.S.A.) had withdrawn his army to the south bank of the Chattahoochee River, at present day Bolton, Georgia, the Sixteen Army Corps, under Federal General Dodge, marched on the 9th from the Sandtown Road one mile east of Marietta. On the 10th, at 3 a.m., the Sixteenth Army corps resumed its march to Roswell.

Back in Roswell Sgt. Mager writes:

This is the first time our brigade was ever camped right in town,... The employes were all women, and there were more of them than we had seen since leaving Nashville, and they were all from the north, were really good looking; most all the women we have seen for the past year have been fearfully homely...According to promise, Gen. Garrard, right away after breakfast this morning, sent a round of whisky. This was the second time we ever had drawn, or ever had whisky issued to us since we entered the service, and we think this was a mistake, as the men never needed it, or asked for it, and always got along just as well without it. The whisky ration was about a gill, and not enough to hurt any one, provided each one just drank his own ration; but there were always in each company some who would never draw their rations at all, which would just leave that much more for somebody else, while among those who did draw their rations there were some who were not content to drink them alone but had a way of gambling 'drink for drink' till some would get a pint, or even a quart, and of course get foolishly drunk. Upon this occasion their delirium took the form of making love to the women, and before night Col. Miller found it necessary to move the brigade a mile north of the town... Our camp north of Roswell was a most beautiful one. Long years ago it had been cultivated till naturally worn out and then abandoned. The ridges and furrows were still plainly visible, and along the ridges had grown numerous pine trees that were now six to eight inches in diameter and 30 to 40 feet high, making the most delightful shade imaginable, which we were needing very much during the heat of the day, as we never felt the sun pour down his rays with such penetrating power before.53 [A mile north of town is the modern area of Alpharetta Street/Norcross Street.]

43

Major-General Grenville M. Dodge
Sixteenth U.S. Army Corps Commander
L.M. Strayer Collection

The Sixteenth Army Corps crossing the Chattahoochee River at the Shallow-Ford. Sketch by George D. Sayller of the Second Iowa Infantry

Frank Leslie's Illustrated Newspaper

Meanwhile, the soldiers of the Federal Fourth Army Corps were busy improving their positions south of the river. Lt. Kyger writes:

...very pleasant this morning; ...Ten a.m., Lieutenant Wolgermuth and myself went blackberrying; have ordered to throw up earth-works to resist an attack if made; I have charge of the working squad.54

Brig. General George Wagner, of the 2nd Div, 4th Army Corps wrote the following for this day:

On the morning of the 10th the line was somewhat changed by throwing forward the left to the next ridge in its front, and connecting with General Kimball's brigade, of the division. In this new position a line of works was constructed by felling trees and covering with earth.55

General Dodge's command, the Federal 16th Army Corps, arrived in Roswell about 1:30 p.m. and passed Colonel Minty's Headquarters, of Garrard's Cavalry, which was in *a fine residence*. Major W.H. Chamberlin of the 81st Ohio Inf. wrote of his regiment's arrival at Roswell:

...having so exhausted the troops by the ascent of a long hill, totally un-protected by shade, that on reaching the summit where there was a woods and shade, our regiment numbered less than eighty men in ranks! nor were other regiments any better. And those who by their iron will did keep in their places, were so nearly exhausted that they, too would have succumbed in a few minutes more if a halt had not been made. Men fell out of ranks then, who had never done so before. I think we never passed through so severe an ordeal in marching.56

Upon reaching the river at the ford, James P. Snell, a member of the 16th Army Corps writes:

The water was very warm. Most of the boys waded in with clothes on—Al-though some doffed pants, socks and boots, and waded in shirt-tail or blouse—but it was slow operation, for the bottom was rough and rocky—hard on bare feet. The teams had to make quite a circuit, but got over in safety. Batry "H" 1st Mo. Lt Arty, alone, of the art'y of our Division, crossed, the rest remained on the west bank, taking position on the hills over-looking the river. We all got across, and into camp, before dark...On the east bank [i.e.south side] of the river there is a narrow bottom of some 50 to 100 yds in width, partly cultivated in corn—on this bottom our ambulance and ordinance trains parked. This flat is bounded on the south by a range of high, steep hills, up which there is no indication of a wagon road—only narrow ravines, defiles and foot-paths. The column went into camp on top of these hills, relieving Newton's Division of the 4th Corps. The 2nd Div. being on the right and Veatch's [4th] Div. on the left.57

[The flat bottom land referred to, is the modern location of the Huntcliff River Stables and the artillery units which took up position in the hills north of the river were: Battery C, 1st Michigan, 14th Ohio Battery, and Battery F, 2nd U.S.]

Pvt;. John Ginste, of the 43rd Ohio Inf., part of the 16th Army Corps. made note of his crossing at the shallowford:

As we were fording the river, waist deep in some places and up to our necks in others, the band of the First Brigade got in the middle of the river on a small island and played several national airs which cheered the men on thru the water.58

As the 16th Army Corps crossed, a 700 foot long pontoon foot bridge was constructed across the river, near the burnt woolen mill site by General Dodge's Pioneer Corps.

While the men were busy at the river, General Dodge sent a message to General Sherman of his arrival.

Headquarters Left Wing, Sixteenth
Army Corps, Roswell, July 10, 1864
- 1:30 p.m.

Major-General SHERMAN:

My troops are arriving and crossing. I have been here three hours, and, in company with General Newton, have thoroughly examined the country. I will occupy and fortify tonight a tete-de-pont half a mile from the river, and extending up and down one mile, covering the entire ford, bridge, and roads leading to them. The ford is half a mile or more in extent, very rough, and impracticable except for troops. To bridge the stream I will have to build over 650 feet in length. I shall use the old piers and trestle between. We have a strong picket out three miles covering the forks of road that leading to McAfee's Bridge, eight miles up the river, and covering the forks of roads that lead to Atlanta. It is too far out to take the command until the river is easily passed by artillery and trains.

G.M. DODGE
Major-General.59

Brigadier General James C. Veatch
Sixteen U.S. Army Corps
Fourth Division Commander
The Photographic History of the Civil War, 1911

Captain John W. Tuttle writes:

We were relieved by troops belonging to the 16th A.C. a little before dark and
retired about half a mile where we went into bivouac for the night.60

After the men of the Chicago Board of Trade Battery
finished swimming in the Chattahooche River, they were relieved
at 4 p.m. by Captain Goodspeed's Battery A, 1st Ohio, part of
Newton's Division. The Chicago Battery limbered up and went
back into camp, in town. Brig. General James Veatch, Commander of the Fourth Division, part of Dodge's Corps, was sick
during his unit's stay in Roswell, and stayed in Dr. Pratt's home.
[Now called "Great Oaks" on Mimosa Blvd.] General
McPherson's quarter-master stores set up on the property of Dr.
Pratt's.

With the larger number of troops in the Roswell area, Mr.
Dunwody's home [now "Mimosa Hall" on Bulloch Ave.] and the
"Bricks" [both two story buildings on Sloan St.] were added with
the Presbyterian Church as hospitals.

Another military event, of lesser importance, but with a
humorous report, occurred west of Roswell. Captain Vale
reported:

In one of our scouting expeditions up the river, about the 10th, some of the
seventh Pennsylvania succeeded in making a bad stampede in the column. We
had halted overnight near a plantation house, where there were a large number
of sceps of bees. Now, the boys always liked honey, and the labor of those bees
was not only appropriated, but their future usefulness as honey producing
colonies sadly marred. We started the next morning on the march before
daylight, and some of the seventh Pennsylvania boys contrived to get a forage
bag over one of the hives, thus securing both bees and honey for future use,
smuggled it into the column, and by supporting it on the horse in front, relieved
each other in turns, and having covered with an overcoat of something of the
kind, carried it along until well in the forenoon. Somehow, the bees maddened
by the jolting and confinement, rushed out in an angry swarm, attacking
indiscriminately officers, men, and horses. Well, for a time it looked as though
the sand-fly experience was to be repeated, and the division scattered all over
the southern Confederacy. But by getting far enough away from the hive, now
left by the purloiners in the middle of the road, after a good deal of scare, and
a good many 'stings' and arrows of outraged fortune, 'the column renewed its

march in pretty fair order. The only casualties noted, and that on the quarter-master's report of Company G, Seventh Pennsylvania Cavalry, was 'one horse stung to death by bees.' This was the literal fact. The bees seemed to center on one particular horse of that company and absolutely stung him to death.61

Back near Roswell and south of the burnt river bridge, Brig. General T.W. Sweeny, Second Division Commander of the Sixteenth Army Corps, had a heated argument with his surgeon. James P. Snell writes:

The Hdqrs. of our Div. are on top of the big hill...Genl. has "an affair" this p.m. with Dr. Gray, Surg. in chief, left wing 16th A.C., in relation to the ambulance the general has for his own private use. The Dr. said it has got to haul sick and the gen'l said it should not, refused to give it up; they had high words and almost an affray, as both had hands on revolvers.62

Meanwhile back in Marietta, Georgia, General George Thomas, Commander of the Army of the Cumberland, writes General Sherman:

The Roswell Factory hands, 400 or 500 in number, have arrived at Marietta. The most of them are women. I can only order them transportation to Nashville where it seems hard to turn them adrift. What had best be done with them?63

Sherman replied:

I have ordered General Webster in Nashville to dispose of them. They will be sent to Indiana.64

For the present time the mill workers are confined on the ground of the Georgia Military Institute, now the site of the Marietta City Club on Powder Springs St. On this day, William King, [Barrington King's brother], living in Marietta, writes in his diary about the depredation committed in Roswell and about his contact with the Federal Soldiers:

...while in town I met Mr. Eldridge and Mr. Bonfoir, [the superintendent of the Roswell Cotton and Wool factories], they inform me of the sad condition of things at Roswell, that the factories had been utterly destroyed and they and all the operatives, men and women, had been arrested and were in Marietta or

Brigadier General Thomas W. Sweeney,
16th U.S. Army Corps, 2nd Division Commander
The Photographic History of the Civil War, 1911

their way to the north, that with the exception of Brother Pratt's house, everyone of the houses of the resp. settlers of Roswell had been broken upon and plundered and everything of value had either been taken away or destroyed and done almost entirely by the 'operatives,' that the soldiers had committed few depredations. What a comment on the human character... Today closes one week since I have been under Yankee [torn]. I thank God that my experiences far exceed sanguine anticipations. I have suffered little annoyance, exclusively of the robbing by the stragglers last Sabbath. I have suffered no more from the soldiers of the Federal Army than those of our own Army. I have mingled and conversed freely with officers and privates. I have not yet met a single individual whose deportment and language has not been gentlemanly, nor a word nor opinion has been expressed to me in the least discourteous manner. Although many cases our opinions materially differed, we pleasantly discussed them. And greatly to my surprise, even among the common soldiers with whom I have also conversed freely, I have seen exhibited no exultant spirit not expressed at our army having so constantly fallen back; but more a spirit of sympathy, for us, and simply a desire to avoid any expression which may be painful to me. All which I have seen compels me to admire the men—they do not seem to feel any hatred toward us, but speak favorably of our army and our people, they say we are one people, the same language, habits and religion, and ought to be one people, they have a higher opinion of the people in the south than before the war; and I am sure even an ultra So. Carolinian can never again say that one So. Ca'n can whip 5 Yankees, to have effected such a change of sentiment North and South towards the people of both sections, has been one of the favorable results of this sad war.65

Meanwhile, the Confederate Cavalry was keeping its eye on Sherman's Left flank:

> Headquarters Kelly's Division
> near Cross Keys, July 10, 1864
> -6 p.m.

Maj. E.S. BURFORD
  Assistant Adjutant General:
  Major: I have the honor to inform you that I have just arrived at this point with Dibrell's brigade. Colonel Hannon reports all quiet in his front; he also reports the force which crossed at McAfee's Bridge to have withdrawn to within half a mile of the bridge, leaving only a small force this side of the river. Colonel Gaines reports the enemy in the vicinity of Roswell to have erected fortifications. Their force is cavalry. I am establishing a courier line from this point to corps headquarters, passing by way of Buck Head.
> Very respectfully,
> J.H. KELLY
> Brigadier-General, Commanding.66

William King
Georgia Archives Vanishing Georgia Collection

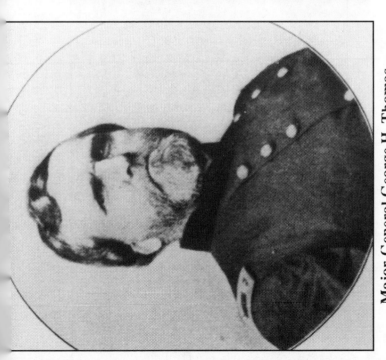

Major-General George H. Thomas
Commander of the U.S. Army of the Cumberland
The Photographic History of the Civil War, 1911

Georgia Military Institute, Marietta, Ga. Established 1851.
Destroyed by Federal Troops in 1864.

Harper's Weekly August 1864

At 8 p.m., from Roswell, General Dodge sent a message to General Sherman:

Roswell, July 10, 1864 - 8 p.m.

Major-General SHERMAN:

Forces are all over river, hard at work fortifying. Have got batteries over also; have built a float bridge. The road bridge is a pretty big job, but will work hard on it. No force in my front that we can hear of.

G.M. DODGE
Major-General.67

Colonel Long, of the Second Brigade, Second Cavalry Division reports of an incident north of Roswell.

Lieut. P.B. Lewis of Third Ohio Volunteer Cavalry, and topographical engineer on my staff, was captured at Alpharetta, Ga., together with 4 of the brigade scouts, by a company of rebel cavalry.68

[Alpharetta, Ga. is located 5 miles north of old down-town Roswell.]

Monday, July 11

About 10 a.m. the 39th Ohio Inf., part of the 16th Army Corps, crosses the river to join the rest of the corps. Pvt. George H. Cadman wrote of that crossing:

The day was very hot, and the sun came down with such force that I cannot think of now without wilting. During our short march into camp I got sunstroke and for several hours the boys say I was crazy. Our doctor came and gave me some morphine, and afterwards whisky & laudenum and got me into a good sleep...have no pain at all, but there is a strange dreamy feeling over me which makes me fear my brain is affected for a time.69

Pvt. John Brobst of the 25 Wisconsin Inf. Regiment,16th Army Corps, was also having his problems with the heat. He wrote,

It is very warm here. A person can not take any comfort in the shade. It is as warm in the shade as it is up there in the sun. We had several men sun struck on the way here, but I am all right yet...70

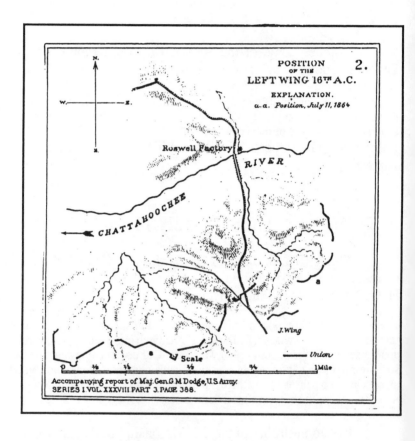

**Sketch of the 16th Army Corps position in
Roswell on July 11, 1864**
The Official Military Atlas of the Civil War

General Newton receives orders at 11:30 a.m. to start moving his division back to the north side of the river. Within an hour the troops are in motion. Captain John W. Tuttle writes:

Lay in same place until about noon when we recrossed the river on a foot bridge constructed since we crossed it before. Went in bivouac in a pleasant shade near Roswell and remained during the remainder of the day and over night.[71]

Lt. Kyger wrote the following of his experiences this day:

...had orders to move at 12.n. Crossed the river on a foot-bridge; halted on a nice ridge one-half mile south of Roswell, at two p.m., with orders that we would not move farther to-night. Very hot; all quiet. R.J. Hasty and myself went to look at the town. Found the ruins of three factories on the banks of a nice rapid stream, Vickery Creek; the largest one was four stories high; all wood-work burned out and the machinery scattered over the ground as it would fall when the wood burned from under it. The most extensive fire was Baron and King. King left but a few days before the *Yankees* burned his factories... the men he had left were arrested. The capacity of the different factories was great enough to employ twelve hundred hands. There are still about four hundred women that have not been sent North.[72]

The only other event in town occurred at some stables, near the Presbyterian Church, where Dr. Cole kept his horses. Dr. Cole wrote:

...our darkies found a large lot of hidden stores in the stable to-day.[73]

Back down at the river, James Snell writes:

General Dodge's Hdqrs. is down by the factory, which with the bridge, was burned down the day before we arrived, the burning of the former threw some 700 girls out of employment. These three large factories, which were burned by our troops by order of the comd'g General have been of great service to the Confederacy—but will no more! In connection with this, is the action of Gen. Dodge, who told Surg. Ashton [7th Iowa] in charge of hospitals in Marietta, to hire as many of these women as he could, as nurses, with pay, rations, etc., allowed such, by the Army regulations. He also put his hand in his pocket, and drew out a $100 bill, and gave it to the hosp. Steward saying; *Take this, and use it in paying for the washing of clothes, etc. of the sick and wounded of our command.* Gen. G.M. don't put on any style in the field. Rides along the column, and around the lines, in a private's blouse, often without shoulder-straps, and sometimes without a staff officer, or an orderly.74

While General Dodge was supervising the construction of the rebuilding of the bridge, south of Roswell, General Sherman wrote to him his feelings about that bridge.

I know the bridge at Roswell is important and you may destroy all Georgia to make it good and strong.75

General Dodge replied,

...I had no fear about being able to build the bridge, but thought you might expect it finished sooner than possible, as it was twice as long as I expected to find it, and twice as long as the river is wide down at Sandtown. I have over 1,000 men at work on it day and night, and it is already well under way. I have planking for floor now on the ground, and not one minute shall be lost in pushing it forward. Every man that can work on it shall be kept at it.76

An artillery fort was built above the burnt Roswell Factory [on the south end of the hill bordered by Vickery Creek, Riverside Drive, and Indian Spring Drive.] It is believed this fort was built to protect the men as they built the bridge and possibly used to guard the bridge, for a short while after McPherson's Army left Roswell. Some soldiers that were not busy on construction details looked for food. Pvt. John Ginste, of the 43rd Ohio Infantry, whose unit was guarding the south end of the bridge, wrote:

Here we found plenty of fruit. Plenty of barrels of corn, rye and wheat and plenty of starches which was manufactured here.77

Other soldiers took time to clean themselves. Pvt. John Brobst of the 25th Wisconsin Inf. Reg. wrote:

I went to work and washed my clothes, and you may believe they needed it bad enough, as we have to go a long time that we can't get a chance to wash any. I have had to go thirty days without a change of clothes, marching in the dirt and sweating, and you can well imagine how we look in such cases...78

Corporal Charles Wright of the 81 Ohio Inf. wrote about one mode of washing,

Take a bar of soap and wade in where the water was running swiftly and about three feet deep; then saturate your clothing with soap, then rub; the swift water would carry away the dirt, and in this way the person and clothes were all washed at the same time.79

On a reconnaissance south of Dodge's entrenchments, Sgt. Mager, of Garrard's cavalry wrote:

...Company I was sent over the river to picket in front of the infantry, and to scout towards Atlanta. In our rounds we ran onto a small building full of medical stores, among which were 1,000 pounds of the nicest corn starch we ever saw. It was all done up nicely in four-pound packages, all of which we strapped to our saddles. There were bushels of blackberries everywhere, and so long as our corn starch lasted no Roman Emperor ever fared more sumptuously than we did. A gallon of well cooked blackberries thickened with a few ounces of corn starch made the most delicate pudding we have ever tasted.80

Pvt. Jesse B. Luce, in the Fourth Army Corps, marched with his infantry Regiment up to Roswell and wrote:

Permission was given to the boys to forage. The town was pretty near deserted by its inhabitants. Gardens were stripped by the soldiers of their contents.81

As General Newton's Division recrossed the river and moved into Roswell to camp, the Second Brigade of Garrard's Cavalry...moved camp to the Old Alabama Road, where it is intersected by the Roswell and Cumming Road, and continue encamped at the place.82 [Modern intersection of Alpharetta Hwy and Holcomb Bridge Rd., two miles north of old Roswell.]

That night back down on the north side of the river, Lt. George Hurlbert, of the 14th Ohio Battery writes of the condition his unit is now in.

It is now nine in the evening. Our army desk is outdoors, and by the light of a flaring candle I have hastily written these few lines. It is thought the battery will cross the river in the morning. I hope then we shall remain in position for a day or two, as the men and horses as well, are worn down by the fatigues of the continued campaign. It is terribly warm during the day, with dusty roads. We cannot move but a short distance as men give out and fall down in the road. Horses are dying at a rapid rate from excessive work. They are left to die where they fall unless someone is kind enough to kill them.[83]

Tuesday, July 12

General Newton's division is up early and starts marching out of Roswell, back to its old camp site on Rottenwood Creek. Capt. John W. Tuttle writes:

Marched about 7 this morning. Our regiment was rear guard and we had a tough time with wagon trains and stragglers.[84]

Work on the bridge still continued. General McPherson moved the 15th Army Corps toward Roswell, coming from Nickajack Creek during the afternoon and camped that night a few miles south of Marietta. John Nourse, camped with the Chicago Board of Trade Battery in town wrote:

I cooked a boiled dinner today—hot work—we captured ten gallons of tanners oil today, and this afternoon I oiled my harness, washed my clothes and got ready to move.[85]

While small, peaceful chores were taking place, one of a more hazardous nature was performed by some men in the Seventy-Second Indiana.

On July 12th Company H was sent about six miles north to a place called Alpharetta for a load of charcoal for blacksmithing purposes. While out on a picket at that place, private Joseph Price was shot by a bushwhacker. He didn't hit Price, but his mare, which was standing by his side was struck in the stifle joint; and although they scoured the woods and brush over and over, they failed to find the rascal who did the shooting, and luck for him that they didn't find him. Price was very much chagrined at having to leave his mare, as he had been riding her ever since we were mounted at Murfreesboro, Tenn., in 1863.[86]

Meanwhile, in Marietta, the Eighty-Seventh Indiana Vol. Inf. and One Hundredth Indiana Vol. Inf. were guarding the

Roswell mill workers. Theodore F. Upson, of the One Hundredth Indiana writes:

We have some 400 young women in the old Seminary building near town. They have been working in a factory at Roswell making cloth for the Confederate Government. The factories were destroyed and the girls are to be sent South or North whichever way they want to go. Some of them are tough and it's a hard job to keep them straight and to keep the men away from them. General Sherman says he would rather try to guard the whole Confederate Army, and I guess he is right about it.87

Back near Roswell, Lt. George Hulburt of the 14th Ohio Battery made the following comment about the fate of the mill employees.

Many of the women are going north. It is to be regretted that women and children must suffer. If the south persists in this struggle, they will be completely ruined.88

Wednesday, July 13

Went blackerrying this afternoon—Hot—as all July days are in Georgia,89 wrote John Nourse.

General Dodge sent a message to Sherman informing him the telegraph at his end was finished, by 3:30 p.m. General Logan's 15th Army Corps was marching for Roswell. A member of the 103rd Illinois Vol. Inf. made the following note about that day's march on the Roswell Road: [GA 120]

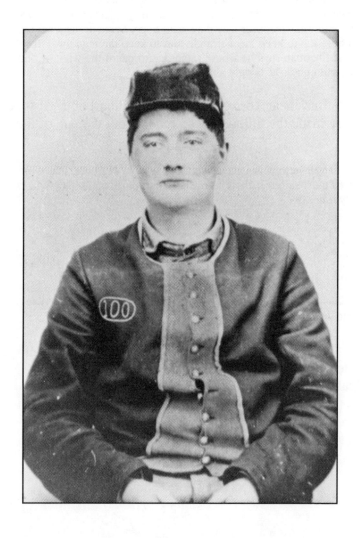

Unknown Private of the 100 Indiana Volunteer Infantry
Library of Congress

Major-General John A. Logan
Fifteenth U.S. Army Corps Commander
The Photographic History of the Civil War, 1911

We marched about 14 miles today. I would rather be in a fight, than endure such a day's march, and I think fighting lacks very much, as deserving to rank as an amusement. I saw a number of cases of congestion of the brain, and a few had real sun-stroke. Saw one poor fellow in a grave yard between two little picketed graves, who I made sure he was gasping his last. Some heartless fellow made a remark as we passed about his luck in getting sun-struck so near good burying facilities. After one heat of only 3 miles the Regt. had fallen out but about 50 men, and we had more than any other in the Brig. If we had been given one hour more in rests, we would not have lost a man.90

By sundown, elements of the 15th Army Corps arrived at their camp, *in a fine meadow,* a half mile west of Roswell. Thaddeus H. Capron, an officer in the 55th Illinois Inf. wrote:

The men were very tired, having been up and marching nearly all night before.91

General Logan, upon reaching Roswell, set up his headquarters in Dr. Pratt's home. ["Great Oaks" on Mimosa Blvd.]
The bridge, across the river, made of *round poles and logs,*92 was completed by nightfall. General Dodge writes:

...a good, substantial double-track trestle road bridge, 710 feet long and 14 feet high, was built by the pioneer corps of, and details from, the command...the skill and cheerful industry displayed by the men in building the bridge [over which the entire Army of the Tennessee crossed with all its trains,] entitles them to much credit, and proves that our gallant soldiers are equal to any and every emergency. The plan, stability, and workmanship of the bridge reflect much credit upon the pioneer corps of the command. The ninth Illinois Mounted Infantry opened communication, on the south side of the Chattahoochee, with the Twenty-Third Army Corps.93

Thursday, July 14

General Dodge moves his headquarters to the south end of the bridge to supervise future troop movement over it. Major General McPherson arrived at Roswell and set up his headquarters with General Dodge. Upon arrival he sent a message to Sherman.

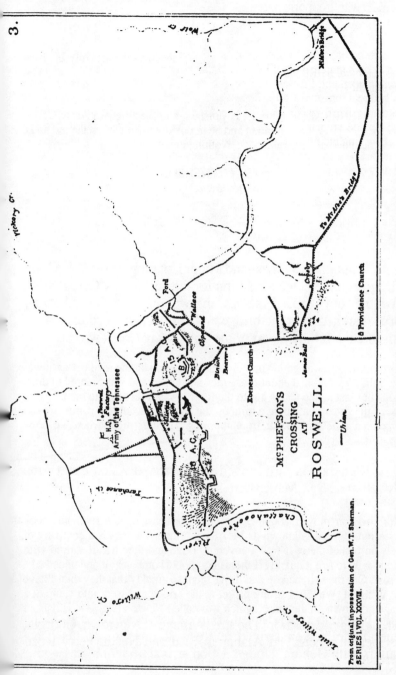

Sketch of the 15th and 16th Army Corps' Position in Roswell, Ga. on July 14, 1864
The Official Military Atlas of the Civil War

65

Roswell Bridge, July 14, 1864
Major-General SHERMAN,
Commanding:

GENERAL: The bridge is finished, and the fifteenth Army Corps will cross the river this afternoon and be in position by night, on the left and a little in advance of General Dodge. Nothing new here.

Jas. B. McPHERSON
Major-General[94]

Captain C.B. Reese and Major Hotaling, of the U.S. Corps of Engineers, selected a position for the 15th Army Corps, to the left of the 16th Corps. As soon as this was reported, the 15th Army Corps marched over the bridge and entrenched. A soldier in the 12th Indiana Infantry, part of the 15th Army Corps wrote:

This morning we was gotten up quite early. We was on the road before it was very light. We marched about four miles and halted and was ordered to draw rations but just as the teams got to the Regt., we was ordered to march again crossed the river went about a mile up the river and went into camp. We did not have a mouthful to eat from morning till after night when we drew rations.[95]

General Garrard moved his cavalry division east of the Roswell area. Sgt. Mager writes:

...our division moved about eight miles northeast up the river and took possession of what is known as McAfee's bridge. There was a company of rebels on picket there. It was a covered bridge and they had it stuffed with cotton ready to fire it quickly if the yanks should come near it and under-take to cross. Our men slipped up and drove them so quickly that they didn't have time to fire it. We left a strong picket at the bridge and went into camp at a village not down on the maps, which was called Newton [sic], and consisted of a house and cross roads.[96] [The small village of Newtown, Georgia, was located where Old Alabama Road and Nesbit Ferry Road intersect.]

Major-General James B. McPherson
Commander of the U.S. Army of the Tennessee
The Photographic History of the Civil War, 1911

At 8 a.m., the Chicago Board of Trade Battery writes:

...we moved out of Roswell and camped five miles from McAfee's bridge, having moved N.E., our guns lay at the Lebanon Mills, said mills are being torn down to repair bridge over Big Bear Creek. Gen. Sherman has removed all the families and factory girls from Roswell to Marietta ...Very hot as usual, but we moved slowly and did not sweat the horses—plenty of fresh oats, and wheat and three quarts of grain for the horses.[97]

[Big Bear Creek is now called Big Creek or Vickery's Creek. The Lebanon Mills: one flour mill owned by the Roswell Manufacturing Company and an Extensive Tannery owned by John Dunwody of Roswell. The mills were located just north of where Old Holcomb Bridge Road and Big Creek intersect.] The Seventeenth Corps signal detachment arrived in Roswell and Lieutenants Worly and Allen were relieved by General Garrard to report to their unit.

Back in Marietta, William King made a visit to the mill employees.

In the afternoon I went to town to make a few visits, the rain interrupting me in part. I saw several of the Roswell factory operatives, Mr. Wood among the number on their way to the North,...[98]

South of Roswell, James Snell wrote of a killer storm that moved in to the area about nightfall.

One of these storms peculiar to the south, favored us this evening commenced about dusk, and lasted about 3/4th of an hours, and was very severe. There was but little rain, but a high wind raged the while, and the 'fitful flashes' of the electric fluid was almost continuous, and so bright as to be almost blinding. It was very destructive: one negro was killed and one white man w'd. of the Pioneer Corps of our Div.;—two men killed and eleven wounded [all of one co.] of our 18th Mo. Inft. Vols. in Veatch's Div., —one man of our Div. train was wounded and another tumbled unceremoniously down hill; at Gen. Dodge's Hdqrs. one horse was killed, and one wounded; Capt. Armstrong of our Div. Pioneer Corps lost three mules; —and 3 men of the 2nd U.S.Arty of the 4th Div. were instantly killed. There were other casualties. but these are all that have come to my knowledge. Situated as we were, so exposed, on a hill top, it seems strange to me that we escaped unharmed.[99]

Lebanon Mill at Vickery's Creek. The Camp of the 2nd U.S. Cavalry Division is to the left of the Mill. Sketch made by Pvt. Charles Holyland of the Chicago Board of Trade Battery.
Courtesy of Charlie Salter

Surgeon John Moore, Medical Director added:

some 4 or 5 men were killed, and about 30 more or less paralyzed. In many cases stacks of arms were struck, and the guns broken and destroyed.100

Pvt. Chadman wrote of this event:

...three men of the Regular Battery, belonging to our Brigade were killed by the lightning striking an oak tree and falling it on them. One man of the 64th Illinois which is also in our brigade was likewise killed during the storm by the lightning. These men had been through all the hardships and perils of our long and fearful campaign and were lying in peace and fancied security to be cut off without a moments warning...101 (See Appendix B.)

Friday, July 15

In Marietta, a correspondent for the New York Tribune writes:

The refugees from the Sweetwater Factory and from Roswell are going North by train as fast as transportation can be afforded. Meantime, Major Tompkins, of General Stoneman's staff, who is charged with the care of these multitudes of homeless people, is looking after their comfort, and under orders from General Sherman, is issuing to them rations ample for their sustenance; they have nine days' supplies given to them when they leave this place.102

Meanwhile, many Federal soldiers south of Roswell were taking a much needed break. A soldier in the 103rd Illinois Vol. Infantry, part of the 15th Army Corps, writes:

This is a glorious place. The current in the river is very swift, and it is the nicest stream to bathe in imaginable. I've a mind to stay here and have my meals brought to me. Expect we will catch some nice fish after they get over being scared at have so many Yanks bobbing around them. It is too hot to write, and altogether too hot to enjoy good health. except in swimming.103 It was also stated a soldier of the 48th Ills. drowned while bathing in the Chattahoochee. (See Appendix C.)

A lot of men were just too tired to move around at all. Pvt. Cadman of the 39th Ohio Inf. observed,

It seems so strange lying here in camp without any noise or bustle. Now the excitement of battle has been over for a few days the men have cooled down and are quiet as mice. At this present time though there some thousands of men lying round here you can scarcely hear a voice, nothing but the sound of the blacksmiths hammer, the singing of birds and the humming of insects. The silence seems painful and unnatural to me. The Thunderstorm of last night seemed far more natural than this silence, after what we have gone through the last 3 months.104

Soldiers that were not idle were working on the fortifications, south of the river. A member of the 12th Indiana Infantry wrote:

Today we did not get our works quite done today. I was around to our right to the 16th corps and they have got good works put up.105

The 1st Ohio Cavalry, detailed by General Garrard, reports to Major-General McPherson for the purpose of guarding the wagons at the river. North/East of Roswell, the men from the Chicago Board of Trade Battery spent their day grazing their horses in the oatfields and picking berries to eat before the day got too hot. The 72nd Indiana and 123rd Illinois, of Garrard's command, went on a scouting patrol, Sgt. Mager writes:

This morning at five o'clock our regiment and the 123rd Illinois, all under command of Lieut.-Col. Biggs, 123rd Illinois, left camp and moved straight for the river at McAfee's Bridge, crossed it and turned directly south for Atlanta. After going 12 miles we struck the rebels in force at Crosskeys, formed line of battle and skirmished with them for two or three hours, capturing a few prisoners without loss to ourselves. Near here we saw marks of ignorance that, up to this time, we had supposed were hardly possible in a free country. On our way we passed a log cabin; standing at the fence was a man whose looks indicated him to be fourscore years old. We asked how far it was to Atlanta. He said he had never been there but guessed it was about 16 miles. *How long have you lived here?* he was asked. *Ever sense I kin rie' leek*, he replied. *How far is it to Crosskeys? I don't know*, he replied; and yet this man was not a fool. Soon after passing his house we saw by the side of the road a large chestnut tree. It had been peeled on the side next to the road and

Second U.S. Artillery. Battery F of this unit took casualties

two large crossed keys cut in the wood, and under them were cut three notches; all of which we rightly interpreted, three miles to Crosskeys. Near the place we saw a large guide board with the letters Roswell painted upon it, and on the post under it were eight deeply cut notches, which of course, meant eight miles to Roswell. We saw many such signs afterwards...we got back to camp just at sundown.106 [Crosskeys is at the modern intersection of Ashford Dunwoody Road and South Johnson Ferry Road.]

Saturday, July 16

This morning, writes John A. Nourse from the Lebanon Mills,

...the first section was ordered out without the caissons, they harnessed but did not move our [out] of camp, they were very glad not to go, as it was very hot, and the roads very dusty...There is a rumour [sic] that we move in the morning—the whole army moves tomorrow.107

Just south of the river, a small incident occurred at General Sweeny's headquarters. James Snell wrote:

...the general...got 'riled up' considerable, and gave 'Bob' Gibson, one of the clerks a particular 'cussing,' on account of Lt. Davis' horse getting loose, and making straight up to the door of the tent, and drinking out of his water bucket. Gibson, who is taking care of the horse in the Lieutenants absence, had just got to the horse to lead him away, when the following celleguy ensued:-

Gen'l-"Whose horse is that?"
Gibson- "Lieut. Davis'"
Gen'l (very mad and red in the face.)- "Who takes care of him?"
Gibson- "I am, while he is gone."
Gen'l (excitedly)- "Why in hell don't you do it then. Take him away! Do you hear? "(At this point, Gibson, very white in the face, takes hold of the latter to lead him away, while the gen'l gives the quadruped a kick on the stern.)
Gibson lead the horse away, and secured him to a tree, and came back to our tent. The general sent the sergeant of the guard to arrest him, and we all expected to see him tied up by the thumbs, as is often done; but the serg't took him to the general's tent, *who made* him go after a fresh pail of water, and then let him go, without further molestation. This little affair shows the *calibre* of the man who has control of six thousand better men. It is nothing now, however—yet we cannot be mortified and indignant... It is such things as these that makes me disgusted with the army and long to be out of it.108

Just to the east of Sweeny's headquarter's, men of the 15th Army Corps, were busy finishing their fortifications and enduring the heat. A soldier in the 12th Indiana Infantry,15th Army Corps writes:

I don't think we will leave here for a while. It is so warm that it hurts the men worst to march than it does to fight.109

Another soldier in the 15th Army Corps had other thoughts on his mind. Pvt. Henry Orendorff of the 103rd Illinois writes:

I suppose you have seen an account of the capture of the factory at Rosswell [sic} and the 500 women, I just wish they would issue them to us soldiers. I believe they sent them back to Marietta, I wish our Regt was back there on Provo Duty...110

Another soldier, Pvt. William Miller, of the 75th Indiana Vol. Inf. did observe some of the mill hands being shipped north. His account was made while he was on a railroad siding at Kingston, Georgia.

We passed a large train loaded with refugees or citizens going north to where they can live until the war is over. They are a poor ignorant set.111

McPherson, after receiving an order that he was to start moving his army the next day, sent a message to Sherman:

Roswell Bridge, July 16, 1864

Major-General Sherman:

I shall have to leave with my trains near this place at least three good regiments and one regiment of cavalry. I am waiting for Garrard to come to obtain some definite information about the road. As far as I can learn yet the Hightower trail is not practicable for troops.

Jas. B. McPHERSON
Major-General.112

Brigadier General John W. Fuller
First Brigade Commander of the 16th U.S. Army Corps
The Photographic History of the Civil War, 1911

At 10:30 P.M. General Dodge issued Special Field Order No. 39:

> Hd Qrs. Left Wing 16th A.C.
> Roswell, Ga. July 16th, 1864
> Special Field Orders No. 39

In order to carry out the instructions of the Dept. of the Tenn. the following movements will be made.

1st - The 4th Div. Brig. Gen. J.W. Fuller, will have the advance, following the 15th A.C.

2nd - The 2nd Div. will follow the 4th Div. and furnish rear guard to the train, of one regiment.

3rd - Hd. Qrs. and Fd. Ordn trains. One wagon on Inft'ry ammunition to a reg't will follow each Division.

4th - There will be taken 40 rounds ammunition in cartridge- boxes, and 60 rounds in wagons, and 2 wagon-loads of artillery ammunition to each Battery, which with reg't'l trains, will follow 2d Div.

5th - Brig. Gen. Fuller will detail one reg't to be kept at the works at the head of the bridge on north side of the river. Instructions to be given the Comd'g Officer from Headquarters.

> By order of Maj. Gen. G.M. DODGE,
> [Sd] J.W. Barnes
> A.A.G.[113]

To this order was added Special Field Order No. 69 fro̅ General McPherson:

> Special Field Orders, No.
> Roswell Bridge, G
> July 16, 18

VII. In order to carry out the spirit and intention of Special Field Orders, Ṇ 35, Headquarters Military Division of the Mississippi, the following moᵛ ments will take place:

1. The fifteenth Army Corps, Maj. Gen. John A. Logan commanding, ᵥ move out from its present position at 5:30 a.m. tomorrow on the road lead to Cross Keys, following this road to a point near Providence Church, wh he will take a left-hand road [sometimes called the upper Decatur road] ;

proceed on this until he reaches Nancy's creek, where he will take up a good position on each side of the road and go into bivouac.

2. The left wing, Sixteenth Army Corps, Maj. Gen. G.M. Dodge commanding, will follow immediately after the Fifteenth Corps on the Cross Keys road to Nancy's Creek, where he will take up a good position on each side of the road and go into bivouac. He will direct the Ninth Illinois Mounted Infantry to feel out from his right for Major-General Schofield's command, and will endeavor to keep open a line of communication by means of vedettes. The pickets of the Fifteenth and Sixteenth Corps should connect.

3. Maj. Gen. F.P. Blair, on his arrival at the bridge with his command, will follow the rest of the army, and report to the Major-General commanding for special instructions.

4. Brigadier-General Garrard, commanding cavalry division, will move his command at 5:30 a.m. tomorrow, crossing McAfee's Bridge, and will push out to the vicinity of Buchanan's, near the headwaters of Nancy's Creek, and take up position covering the roads to his left and front. He will also feel to the right and open communication with the Fifteenth Army Corps. He will also leave a sufficient guard for McAfee's Bridge, and one regiment to be stationed near Roswell to form part of the guard for trains and to patrol the country in the vicinity. The trains will be compactly parked, in the most secure position which can be found, as near the bridge as practicible.

5. Each corps commander will leave one good regiment of infantry to form the guard for the train. The regiment from the Sixteenth Corps will take post at the bridge on the west side, and the other two regiments, one from the Fifteenth and one from the Seventeenth will remain immediately with the trains.

6. Great vigilance must be exercised by the guard to prevent the train from being surprised by the enemy's cavalry.

7. All wagons and incumbrances not needed for battle must be left behind.

8. The supply train of the cavalry division will be parked with the infantry trains.

> By order of Maj. Gen. James B. McPherson
> Wm. T. Clark
> Assistant Adjutant-General.114

Meanwhile, Major-General F.P. Blair Jr., had his 17th Army Corps in motion for Roswell. The corps marched to within a mile of Marietta and went into bivouac at 11:00 p.m.

Major-General Frank P. Blair, Jr.
Seventeenth U.S. Army Corps Commander
The Photographic History of the Civil War, 1911

Sunday, July 17

General Blair Jr., had his corps up and marching towards Roswell at 4:00 a.m. At 5:00 a.m. General Garrard's cavalry, with the Chicago Board of Trade Battery, saddled up and filed across the Chattahoochee at McAfee's Bridge. The 3rd & 4th Ohio Cavalry stayed at McAfee's Bridge as a guard. The 1st Ohio Cavalry guards the ford closer to Roswell. At 5:30 a.m. the 15th Army Corps started moving out of their entrenchments marching south. From the 15th Corps, the 26th Illinois Infantry and the 31st Iowa Infantry remain on the south side of the river to guard the supply trains on that side. When the end of the 15th Army Corps was two miles from that location, the 16th Army Corps moved out behind it. From the 16th Corps, the 43rd Ohio Infantry was left to guard the supply trains from the north side of the river. The 16th Corps also left behind two artillery guns from the battery C, 1st Michigan, to command a road leading south out of town. General Veatch, who had been staying at Rev. Pratt's home due to his poor health, relinquished the command of his division to General Fuller. One soldier, in the 103rd Illinois Volunteer Infantry, did not like to go so soon after the work that was put into the fortifications; as he wrote:

After erecting some good works at Roswell (the best we have yet built, capable of holding at least 25,000 men) we were provided with three days' rations and cartridges *adlibitum*, for another of what an Augusta paper calls *Sherman leap-frog-like advances.*[115]

The march was not a fast pace, as James P. Snell writes: We marched very slowly, which gave the boys plenty of time to pick blackberries by the roadside, of which there were fine ones in abundance.[116]

The 4th U.S. Cavalry and part of the 9th Illinois Mounted Infantry ride in front of the marching columns to scout for Confederates. According to James P. Snell:

General Joseph E. Johnston (C.S.A.)
The Photographic History of the Civil War, 1911

4 Co's of the 9th Illinois Infantry being in the advance, had quite a skirmish with enemy's dismounted cavalry pickets. Orderly Serg't Turner, Co. 'A', captured one of these isolated *Johnnies*, but was shot dead by him, while taking him into headquarters, by carelessly allowing him to retain his revolver.[117]

About 7 hours later, the lead units of the 17th Army Corps arrive in Roswell. Lt. Henry Speer of the 78th Army Infantry wrote:

[We] marched very rapidly until 1 p.m., when we arrived at Roswell, a small village 18 miles from Marietta, where we stopped and cooked some dinner and had a little rest. Starting again at 5:50 p.m., crossing the river and marched about 3 miles beyond and encamped for the night. (This 23 mile march with equipment, in severe summer heat, with bad food and under arms is unbelievable.)[118]

The Confederate Government was very much disturbed to hear of the Federal Army gaining a position south of the Chattahoochee River, so action was taken.

Richmond, July 17, 1864.
GENERAL J.E. JOHNSTON:

Lieut. Gen. J.B. Hood has been commissioned to the temporary rank of the general under the late law of Congress. I am directed by the Secretary of War to inform you that as you have failed to arrest the advance of the enemy to the vicinity of Atlanta, far in the interior of Georgia, and express no confidence that you can defeat or repel him, you are hereby relieved from the command of the Army and Department of Tennessee, which you will immediately turn over to General Hood.

S. COOPER
Adjutant and Inspector
General.[119]

Back in Marietta, William King made note of what some Roswell Citizens' thoughts were on their present state of affairs.

I wrote to my sister Cate a few days ago, urging them all to move here and stay with me. Today I rec'd a reply from Bro. P. stating that they were now getting on very comfortably, since the factory women had all been sent off, and he

General John Bell Hood (C.S.A.)
The Photographic History of the Civil War, 1911

thought they could safely remain at home as long as the federal Army remained, when they might find it unsafe to remain in Roswell, if so, they move here and stay with me, it would be a comfort for us all to be together, in these sad days.120 (Bro. P. is Rev. Pratt who lived at what is now called "Great Oaks" on Mimosa Blvd.)

By 9:00 p.m. units of the 17th Army Corps were still marching through Roswell to catch up with Gen. McPherson's other two corps, which were now 10 miles away.

Monday, July 18

The Chicago Board of Trade Battery, which is camped nine miles east of McAffe's Bridge, sends four of its guns back to that bridge. John A. Nourse writes:

The two remaining sections went back to the bridge where the second brigade lay in camp. We feed all the wheat and oats the horses can eat. There is plenty in the country, and no one uses it except Uncle Sam's soldiers, potatoes, apples, and berries are plenty. When will this very hot weather end?121 (McAfee's Bridge ruins are just south of the location where Holcomb Bridge Road crosses the Chattahoochee River.)

Confederate scouts are watching these troop movements and others of the Federal Army. Their information is relayed to General Hood, who in turn informs Richmond.

Near Atlanta, July 18, 1864

HON. SECRETARY OF WAR:

The enemy advanced today on all the roads leading from Isham's Ford and Roswell, and established his lines on Peach Tree Creek, his right resting on the Chattahoochee in the vicinity of the railroad, his left at Buckhead; our Army about 4 miles from Atlanta, the creek intervening between Armies.

J.S. HOOD
General.122

QUITE THE REVERSE.

" Johnston has Sherman just where he wants him."—*Richmond Enquirer.*

Cartoon Humor at the Expense of the Confederate Army
Richmond Enquirer

Ruins of McAfee's Bridge as it stands today, facing west.
Holcomb Bridge Road is pictured at the right.
Author's Photo

Tuesday, July 19

General Garrard's Cavalry was being used to guard the extending left flank of Sherman's Army, and at the same time, conducting raids. In view of this manpower shortage, he wrote to headquarters suggesting that McAfee's Bridge be destroyed. Meanwhile, the four guns of the Chicago Board of Trade Battery, the 4th Ohio Cavalry, were ordered to join their command near Stone Mountain. John A. Nourse writes:

This morning we went out and brought in all the oats our horses could eat. We got back to camp at eight o'ck., and then the order was to move and join the command. We waited until the men all came in from foraging, and then at one o'ck we started...123

The 1st Ohio Cavalry was left near Roswell to patrol the area. The 26th Illinois Infantry, which had been guarding the supply trains, south of Roswell, marched toward Decatur to re-join their command. The 9th Illinois Mounted Infantry was ordered to Roswell as a train guard for the 16th Army Corps wagon train.

Wednesday, July 20

The Battle of Peachtree Creek was fought this day, north of Atlanta and ended in a Confederate defeat. Meanwhile, General McPherson wrote Sherman notifying him that General Garrard's headquarters are in Decatur and his command is so disposed as to cover his rear and line of communications back to Roswell. General Sherman, late this night, sent General Garrard a message concerning McAfee's Bridge and the Cavalry's wagons.

> HDQRS, Military Division of the
> Mississippi, In the Field, near
> Atlanta, July 20, 1864-Midnight.

GENERAL GARRARD
Commanding Cavalry Division:

General; After destroying the bridge at McAfee's, which I suppose is already done, you will send to General McPherson's guard at the bridge at Roswell your wagons, lead horses, and baggage, and proceed rapidly to Covington. If the McAfee's Bridge is not already burned you can send a messenger to the guard already there to do it and move to Roswell. This need not delay your departure for Covington at once.

W.T. SHERMAN
Major-General, Commanding.124

Meanwhile, the Hashville Times noted the arrival, in their city, of mill workers from Sweetwater factory. These employees along with the Roswell Employees were all being shipped north to Louisville, Kentucky.

Exile of the Sweetwater Operatives

Monday night, over two hundred men and women were sent to this place from Sweetwater Cotton Factory, and its vicinity, by order of General Sherman. The factory is, or was before General Sherman destroyed it, locate din Campbell County, on this side of the Chattahoochie, or Sweetwater Creek, some fifteen miles from Atlanta. It employed over one hundred and fifty hands, who manufactured Osnaburg, yarns, etc., mostly for the rebel army. The men were exempt from military service, on account of their skill. They are to be sent north of the Ohio River to earn their living during the existence of the war. If they are honest, well disposed people they can readily find employment at excellent wages. These laborers have fared rather better than other classes of people lately. Their fabrics were in great demand, and there was not a store of any kind outside of the large towns, where a yard of cotton goods could be bought. Consequently, the former were all eager to exchange the best of their produce for the factory goods, and the operatives much preferred produce to worthless Confederate money. They were not molested by conscript officers because their work was necessary, and guerrillas dared not rob them, for they were protected by the rebel government. The hands got about $6 per day. The destruction of these factories is a severe loss to the rebels, as a large portion of their military clothing came from Campbell County.125 (Sweetwater Cotton Factory site is now a state park, west of Atlanta.)

Thursday, July 21

General Sherman wrote General McPherson about the wagons of his command and Garrard's.

> HDQRS. Military Division of the
> Mississippi, In the Field, near
> Atlanta, July 21, 1864-1 a.m.

General McPherson
Army of the Tennessee:

I have ordered Garrard to send to Roswell his wagons and impediments and pushing rapidly and boldly on the bridges across the Yellow River and Ulcofauhachee, near Covington to be gone two days. Give orders that in the mean time no trains come up to you from Roswell, he will substantially cover the roads back because all the cavalry in that direction will be driven away...

> W.T. Sherman
> Major-General, Commanding.[126]

Shortly after this message, General Garrard wrote Sherman acknowledging his letter of the 20th.

> HEADQUARTERS CAVALRY DIVISION
> Decatur, July 21, 1864

MAJOR-GENERAL SHERMAN
Commanding Army:

General: I have the honor to acknowledge the receipt of your orders last night at 1:30 a.m. at that time one brigade (three regiments) was at Cross Keys, ten miles from here, with pickets in every direction from three to four miles; one regiment was at McAfee's bridge and one at Roswell, leaving me only five regiments, which were all on duty here guarding the roads...

> K. GARRARD
> Brigadier-General Commanding
> Division.[127]

Meanwhile, attention was given to the Roswell Mill Employees by the *New York Tribune Newspaper*. The article reads,

The same day on which the 23rd corps effected the crossing of the river (the 8th), Col. Garrard's cavalry also crossed at Roswell but about an hour later that this corps. Having marched rapidly, the day before, upon the large cotton factory at that point, he took it altogether by surprise, destroying a vast quantity of the Army canvas, which was extensively manufactured there, and taking captive 400 factory girls. The latter capture was certainly a novel one in the history of wars, and excited not a little discussion as to the disposition which was proper to be made of the fair captives. Giving "Aid and comfort to the enemy" they most assuredly were, and much valuable tent cloth; but in the case of many of them, it was involuntary service, since they had been confined and compelled to labor there without cessation from the breaking out of the Rebellion. Then, too, the cartel makes no provisions touching the exchange of prisoners of this sort, neither would it do to send them across the lines to their former employees, since they would immediately be set to the manufacture of tents again; nor was it as all safe to discharge them unconditionally in the midst of two great armies, many of them far removed from their friends and helpless. Thus red tape was about to become involved in a hopeless entangle-ment with (unreadable) Line, tent cloth and cartels, when General Sherman interposed and solved the knotty question by loading them into one hundred and ten wagons, and sending them to Marietta. to be sent north of the Ohio (River), and set at liberty. Only think of it! Four hundred weeping and terrified Ellens, Susans, and Maggie's transported, in the springless and seatless Army wagons, away from their lovers and brothers of the sunny south, and all for the offense of weaving tent-cloth and spinning stocking yarn! However, I leave the whole business to be adjudged according to its merits by your readers.128

The *New York Times* also made comment to the fate of the Roswell Mills. Their article reads:

The destruction of the Mills at Roswell proves to have been a very severe blow to the Confederates, in addition to the flouring mills, which were very complete and extensive, there were large and well appointed mills for the manufacture of cloths. The regular monthly product of these establishments was 30,000 yards of cotton and 15,000 yards of woolen goods-principally such goods as were used by the Army. The machinery, which was of the best and most approved patterns and inventions, was made at Patterson, New Jersey. The mills were thoroughly destroyed. The operatives, some three hundred women, are thus thrown out of employment, and will be sent north... From the fact that

Johnston left these mills with all the manufactured and raw material accumulated at them is evidence that he did not retire from the Kennesaw line with any great deliberation. The fact alone is sufficient evidence that he deemed his position before Marietta one that he could hold.129

While the New York newspapers were commenting on the Roswell incident in general, the *Louisville Daily Journal* was announcing the actual arrival of the first large group of mill hands to their city.

Georgians bound for the North - A small detachment of the Southern Confederacy in the shape of two hundred and nineteen men, women, and children, arrived in the city last evening on the Nashville train. They are all ardent admirers of Jeff Davis and the Southern cause. They were picked up 'way down in Georgia' by order of Major-General Sherman, and forwarded to this city to be sent north of the Ohio river. to remain during the war. The population of Indiana is on a rapid increase, but we fear that the additions will not add much to the loyalty of the state. The officers in charge of the detachment report that a motley group of the disloyal citizens of Georgia, said to number fifteen hundred of both sexes and of all ages, are now at Nashville, waiting transportation to the land of freedom and drafts beyond the flow of the Ohio. George, thoughtful George, of Capt. Jones office, who never makes a bad guess, thinks that the glory of the South has gone up a spout! We are of about the same opinion.130

Friday, July 22

Four hundred wagons of the 15th and 17th Army Corps have left their river camps, very early in the morning, and are enroute to Decatur. Escorting the trains are the 43rd Ohio Infantry, the two guns from Battery C., 1st Michigan, and five companies from the 9th Illinois Mounted Infantry. The Battle of Atlanta was fought, east of the city, ending in a Confederate defeat.

Portion of first passenger
station, constructed in 1858,
by the L&NRRCo. located at
corner 9th & Broadway, Louisville, Ky.

Louisville Train Depot
Courtesy of Charles B. Castner, L & N Collection

Saturday, July 23

L.M. Dayton, , Aide-de-camp to Sherman, wrote General Logan over his concern of the remaining wagons in Roswell.

> HDQRS. Military Division of the
> Mississippi, In the field, near
> Atlanta, July 23, 1864 - 11:45 p.m.

MAJOR-GENERAL LOGAN
Commanding Army of Tennessee:

General: I am directed by the General Commanding to say that he prefers not to give orders as regards Roswell until he hears further from the Cavalry; in the meantime let your wagons go to the railroad via Pace's Ferry and load at Vining's Station of Marietta such forage as you may need. The general understood yesterday that you had four day's supply.

I am, with much respect,

> L.M. DAYTON
> Aide-de-camp.131

Back near Decatur, General Dodge, concerned for the safety of his supply wagons, reported observations made by Sergeant Childs of the wagons in Roswell and an incident involving a wagon belonging to the 17th Army Corps.

> Headquarters Left Wing,
> Sixteenth Army Corps,
> Near Atlanta, Ga., July 23, 1864

LIEUT. COL. WILLIAM T. CLARK
Assistant Adjutant-General:

Sergeant Childs, Fourteenth Ohio Battery, came through today from Marietta, passing through Roswell at 2 p.m. All our trains were there with light guard. On the direct road to Decatur he passed one wagon belonging to the Seventeenth Corps, Loaded with grain, burning. He came through Decatur; saw no rebels, but heard of them off road. It appears to me that our trains are in great danger. They had not received any orders and did not know what to do.

Very respectfully, your obedient servant,

> G.M. DODGE
> Major-General Commanding.132

Sunday, July 24

General Logan, still in need of his wagons, did not have the extra manpower to escort these supplies safely to Vinings, Ga.; therefore, he again wrote Sherman of his problem.

Before Atlanta, Ga., July 24, 1864

MAJ. GEN. W.T. SHERMAN
Commanding Military Division of the Mississippi:

I have the honor to state the brigade of cavalry from General Sherman's command, which by information from you of last evening, was to report to me this morning, has not yet been reported. It is necessary that trains with forage and rations should be brought forward from Roswell. You are aware that I have no cavalry at my disposal, nor is it practicable to take a sufficient force of Infantry from the lines as a guard to bring up the trains. Shall the Roswell depot be abandoned and all the trains brought forward under guard there stationed, and shall the bridge be destroyed?

Very respectfully, your obedient servent,

JOHN A. LOGAN
Major-General.133

Sherman then sent his reply:

HDQRS. Military Division of the
Mississippi, In the field, near
Atlanta, Ga, July 24, 1864

MAJ. GEN. JOHN A. LOGAN
Commanding Army of the Tennessee:

General: ...You will no longer send your wagons by Roswell, but by Buckhead, and Pace's Ferry , and when you change you will draw from the railroad bridge...

W.T. SHERMAN
Major-General, Commanding.134

General Logan, not getting a clear answer to his problem, ordered part of the 1st Ohio Cavalry, guarding the wagons, to escort them to Vining's Station.

Major-General George Stoneman (U.S.)
Horsemen Blue and Gray, 1960

Monday, July 25

General Stoneman, unaware that most of the 1st Ohio Cavalry had moved out of Roswell, wrote Garrard concerning the replacement of the regiment with a smaller detachment.

General Sherman's Headquarters,
July 25, 1864

GENERAL K. GARRARD,
Commanding Cavalry Division:

General: ...The general says that you can call in the regiment you now have at the Factory bridge, and that you can replace it with such a portion of your command under an officer, as you cannot make available in the contemplated operations. This party need not, nor will it be considered and will act as a sort of flank guard to Marietta, and to hold the bridge for ulterior purposes; in case it may be wanted. An Infantry force will also be sent there from Marietta if necessary.

GEORGE STONEMAN
Major-General.[135]

An Infantry force was sent to Roswell, but not from Marietta. The 14th Illinois Infantry, Company C, in Acworth, Georgia was sent to Roswell and arrived on this day.

General Logan now wrote Sherman of his order to use the cavalry guard, at Roswell, to bring up his wagons.

HDQRS. Department and Army of the
Tennessee, Near Atlanta, Ga.,
July 25, 1864

...I also requested General Garrard to leave that portion of a regiment of his command, part of the guard at Roswell, at that place until the empty teams of his train return to Marietta for supplies could arrive at Roswell and convey the sick to the hospitals at Marietta. All the ambulances of this Army are employed in moving our hospitals to the rear, hence the necessity of availing myself of General Garrard's empty trains.

JOHN A. LOGAN
Major-General.[136]

While attention was being focused on the disposition of the army wagons at Roswell, a reporter for the *Elk Horn Independent*, wrote of his visit to the Roswell Mill Employees, in Louisville, Kentucky.

Last evening, in company with a friend, I went to the Military Prison to see the factory hands from Roswell, Georgia. Through the kindness of the surgeon in charge we were permitted to go through the entire establishment, and if they are a fair specimen of Georgia refugees, I say let the refugees remain in Dixie. Among the whole crowd I found but two Union persons. A more degraded, ignorant, scaley set of men, women and children I never saw. Were they less arrogant and brazen-faced, I should pity them, and in fact went with the intention of pitying the poor, suffering Union refugees, but my sympathy soon sank below zero, and disgust assumed its place. They uttered loud and bitter curses on General Sherman, using language like the following: 'What did you'ns come down thar for and drive we'uns from home?' 'That General Sherman wants to steal our slaves, indeed he du; and he lit all the factries, and didn't leave nothing for we'uns nor our kin. Right smart way to fight, we reckons, drivin' little children and old folks out'er work and vitals, and toteing us way up here.' 'General Sherman is a wolf, a bar, a beast, and our gov'ment will teach him suffing when they find him. Orphans cuss him, Gord (God) cusses him, and the hull South cusses him.'

The above is a fair sample of their garulous loquacity. The men are to be sent north of the Ohio, and the women and children are being sent to various places in the city to work.137

Tuesday, July 26

On this day John A. Nourse, of the Chicago Board of Trade Battery, writes from east of Atlanta:

At 4 o'ck p.m. the pack mules and teams were sent to Roswell.138

The 14th Illinois, Company C, having camped in Roswell, broke camp and marched to Marietta.

Wednesday, July 27

The Richmond Examiner, a Confederate paper, was slow at receiving information of Union troops at Roswell. Not until 17 days after the event did they publish the following article:

The enemy are all quiet, and are chiefly engaged in washing, picking black-berries and resting, and show no evidence of an immediate advance, but seem to be massing their infantry on their left and our right, near Roswell. Slight skirmishing continues across the river, near the burnt bridge. Sherman's and Thomas' headquarters are near Vinings' Station.

Howard has ordered back Gen. Newton, commanding one of his divisions, to the Northside of the river, and Gen. Dodge, commanding the Sixteenth Army Corps, with two small divisions of infantry, immediately crossed to the south side and took Newton's place.

Garrard has one division of cavalry on this side of the Chattahoochee River, in front of Dodge's infantry, on the Buckhead Valley Railroad, distant about three-fourths of a mile from the river, behind temporary breastworks of rails and dirt.[139]

Another article, about the mill workers, appeared in the *Patriot and Union*, a Pennsylvania paper. It reads as follows:

The War Upon Women - a dispatch from Louisville state that another install-ment of fifty Confederate women from Georgia arrived at that place on Friday. Three hundred and fifty more are reported at Nashville on their way to Louisville. They are to be sent out of the limits of the United States.[140]

Back in Marietta, Georgia, William King talked with Federal officers to find out the conditions in Roswell.

About 7 o'clock a company of cavalry under Capt. Shultz connected with Gen. Garrard's Division came up and encamped under the trees, they were just from Roswell and now passing around to the west. One of the Officers told me he saw and spoke to Bro. Pratt yesterday, that a regiment of Infantry had been sent to Roswell to remain on duty there, which would afford them protec-tion.[141]

Thursday, July 28

The battle of Ezra Church is fought west of Atlanta and ends in a Confederate defeat.

In Roswell, most of the men from the Roswell Battalion who had deserted the unit on July 4, 1864, turned themselves into Federal units in the area. The following are those men:

J.M. Anderson	Newton Green
James Barker	Andrew W. Grey
John Burnett	Asel Hindman
James Cobb	Ransom Lindsey
John Coleman	Kinson Ridens
William Coleman	Clinton M. Webb
Andrew J. Copeland	Daniel D. Whelchel
Benjamin H. Dupree	Hiram Whelchel
George W. Eades	Major Whelchel
Isaac Fretwell	Jessee William [142]

These men were then sent to Chattanooga, Tennessee.

Friday, July 29

Andrew Johnson, Military Governor of Tennessee, writes General H. Thomas, a Federal officer in Georgia, about his views of sending southern citizens north.

NASHVILLE, July 29, 1864

Maj. Gen. GEORGE H. THOMAS

Commanding Department of the Cumberland

General Thomas will remember that the Nashville and Northwestern Railroad was placed by the Secretary of War under my control, with authority to select engineers, etc. The road is now used to its utmost capacity. The services of Major Yates at this time are important, and I hope he can be spared, which will not interfere with Colonel McCallum in any way. I hope you will permit me to make one suggestion in reference to persons being sent to Nashville and north of it. The whole population in our front, instead of being sent this way, should be pressed back with the rebel army. Let them hear the cries and suffering, and supply their stomachs and backs with food and raiment. To the extent that we received and feed their population, which is disloyal, we relieve the Confederate Government. Let them fall back with the army. By sending them her they add to the rebel or Copperhead sentiment and increase opposition to the Government. The rebels who have been sent from east Tennessee north, should have been sent south. They would rather go anywhere else than south, and it would create more terror than sending them north. If this meets your views, I hope you will submit to General Sherman for consideration.

ANDREW JOHNSON
Military Governor of
Tennessee.143

Governor Johnson, future president of the United States, made note of the *rebels sent from East Tennessee north*. The area he is referring to is Chattanooga, Tennessee. This is where persons from Georgia were sent first, as in the case of the mill workers.

Saturday, July 30

The following is General Thomas' reply:

Headquarters Department of the
Cumberland, In the Field,
July 30, 1864

GOVERNOR ANDREW JOHNSON
Nashville, Tennessee:

I remember that at first the North-Western Railroad was placed under your charge, but though that subsequently all the military railroads were placed in charge of Colonel McCallum. Major Yates will be detailed to report to you. I have always held the same opinion about sending the rebels and their sympathizers south instead of north that you do, and have frequent conversations on that subject with General Sherman. To send them south as our lines advance would require that they be sent through our lines under flag of truce, which he does not like to do at this time. They will probably all be sent south after the campaign is over.

GEORGE H. THOMAS
Major-General, Commanding.144

Andrew Johnson,
Military Governor of Tennessee and
Future President of the United States.
National Archives

Sunday, July 31

The deserters of the Roswell Battalion arrive in Louisville, Kentucky, from Chattanooga, Tennessee, and take the oath of allegiance at the military prison there. Most of them are then released north of the Ohio River. The rest are released a couple of days later.

Chattanooga Station in 1864 as seen by the mill workers on their way North. Lookout Mountain is in the background.

National Archives

...station in 1864 looking North. From here the mill workers...

August 1864

Monday, August 1

General Sherman issues Special Field Order No. 48 to all his commanders concerning their new lines of operations. General Garrard's cavalry is ordered to relieve General Schofield's Infantry in the trenches, as well as

...to patrol the roads about Decatur, and picket towards Roswell.145

Tuesday, August 2

The river bridge, south of Roswell, is still important to Sherman as shown in the following order.

> HDQRS. Military Division of the
> Mississippi, In the Field, near
> Atlanta, Georgia, August 2, 1864

General THOMAS:

I am quite unwell to-day...Order all bridges above Pace's except that at Roswell, to be destroyed.

> W.T. SHERMAN
> Major-General, Commanding.146

Meanwhile, as the Federal army is shifting its lines around Atlanta, attention is again focused on the Roswell Mill workers. The following article appeared in the *Patriot and Union:*

WAR UPON WOMEN. The New York commercial, a republican paper, makes the annexed just comment upon the course of Gen. Sherman in sending to the north four hundred factory girls who were captured at Roswell, Georgia: 'A newspaper correspondent published a story, which we trust, for the sake of the officer implicated, as well as our own national good name, may prove to be unfounded. It is to the effect that General Sherman, finding at Roswell, in Georgia, four hundred factory girls, employed in a large cotton factory at that point, ordered the whole of the unfortunate creatures to be sent north of the Ohio. Gen. Sherman has shown on two or three occasions that ability as a military commander is quite compatible with something not far removed from imbecility in respect to civil matters. He writes stupendously foolish orders on things political, and is evidently incapable of administering a village on practical principle. But it is hardly conceivable that an Officer, wearing the United States commission of Major General, should so far have forgotten the commonest dictates of decency and humanity (Christianity apart) as to drive four hundred penniless girls hundreds of miles away from their homes and friends to seek a livelihood amid a strange and hostile people. We repeat our most earnest hope that further information may redeem the name of Gen. Sherman and our own from the frightful disgrace which this story, as it now comes to us, must else inflict upon one or the other.[147]

Wednesday, August 3

General Stoneman and General McCook, Federal Cavalry commanders had been sent on roads south of Atlanta, late in July. The raids went badly and the scattered Federal Cavalry made it back to their lines as best as they could. One large group of Federal cavalrymen approached Roswell from the east, while being pursued and attacked by mounted Confederate forces under the leadership of Col. W.C.P. Breckinridge. Due to the previous destruction of McAfee's Bridge, a ford north of that location was found for a crossing. Federal Lieut. Col R.W. Smith wrote in his report:

We struck the Chattahoochee about twenty three miles northeast of Marietta; sun an hour high; found an old but difficult ford, and succeeded in getting the command all over about 9 p.m., and went into camp.[148]

Colonel W.C.P. Breckinridge (C.S.A.)
Active Service by J.B. Castleman, 1917

Modern Photo of the old ford, center foreground, looking west. Here, Col. Smith's Fed. cavalrymen crossed and camped on the opposite shore.

(This old ford is now where East Jones Bridge Road dead ends at the Chattahoochee River, on the east bank. Just 20 feet upstream from the W.W.I era steel bridge site, the cut in the riverbank can still be seen where the horses and men crossed; also, the wartime road on the west-bank can still be seen.)

Thursday, August 4

Lieut. Col. R.M. Smith at the old ford, wrote in his report:

August 4, started at daylight, and arrived at Marietta at 11 a.m.[149]

General Sherman ordered more cavalry to Roswell to strengthen the guard already there, due to the Confederate activity east of that location.

> HDQRS. Military Division of the
> Mississippi, In the Field, near
> Atlanta, Georgia, August 4, 1864

Colonel ROSS
Marietta:

Let Colonel Adams collect all of General Stoneman's cavalry, make his depot at Marietta, and picket Roswell in connection with the regiment of infantry there. I will trust that General Stoneman will fight his way out like General McCook. Tell Colonel Adams to make a minute report of the facts and let me draw conclusions.

> W.T. SHERMAN
> Major-General Commanding.[150]

Sherman was still unaware that General Stoneman had surrendered with a large portion of his command near Macon, Georgia, on July 30.

Back in Pennsylvania, the *Patriot and Union*, printed another article mentioning the mill workers and their feelings towards the Union generals in the field.

—Our Generals out west are very busy sending the ladies back and forth. Sherman sends from Georgia 200 to 300 helpless factory girls north—to starve—while Rosecrans is packing them by the dozens, from Missouri, south. Between the vandalism of Hunter, the barbarity of Sherman and Rosecrans, and the lawlessness of Banks, the country will need peace to keep us all from the horrors of Tartar civilization![151]

Brigadier-General John McArthur
Generals in Blue, 1959

Friday, August 5

Sherman's aide-de-camp, L.M. Dayton, issued an order placing Brig. Gen. John McArthur in

...command of the district of country embracing Kennesaw, Marietta, Roswell, and the west bank of the Chattahoochee River, and the Sweet Water.152

Colonel S. Adams, of the 1st Kentucky Cavalry, writes Capt. L.M. Dayton stating he has sent his command to Roswell, as Sherman ordered.

MARIETTA, AUGUST 5, 1864

Capt. L.M. DAYTON:

I sent all the men of my command that were fit for duty to Roswell Factory, as directed by General Sherman. I have no further news from the remainder of General Stoneman's command. My horses I sent to Roswell are much broken down, and feet worn out for want of shoes. I have more transportation than is necessary, and can have 200 or 300 more men for duty by turning over pack-saddles and mounting on the pack animals. Lieutenant-Colonel Smith, of General Stoneman's command, will report in person this morning to General Sherman.

S. ADAMS
Colonel First Kentucky
Cavalry.153

Meanwhile, William King noted in his diary the news he was able to put together by talking with the surviving Federal raiders, that had passed through Roswell to Marietta.

...Gen'l Stoneman surrendered with the larger portion of his force, a large body however made their escape and retreated by way of Eatonton, Madison, Watkinsville within 4 miles of Athens and Hog Mountain, and passed the Chattahoochee about 2 miles above McAfee's Bridge by a ford, to Roswell. A portion of Wheeler's command in close pursuit of them all the way until they passed the Chatt's River, now and then attacking their rear. I asked the Lut. if they did not travel faster ret'g than going, he said much, taking on 4 hours sleep out of the 24...154

Saturday, August 6

Sherman orders in the guards at Roswell, as the area is now of no great importance.

HDQRS. Military Division of the
Mississippi, In the Field, near
Atlanta, August 6, 1864.

General McARTHUR
Marietta:

You may order the bridge at Roswell to be burned, and draw in the regiment of infantry and cavalry now there; the river being fordable, there is no use in having detachments out exposed.

W.T. SHERMAN
Major-General, Commanding155

Sunday, August 7

The bridge is destroyed and General McArthur informs Sherman.

MARIETTA, GA. AUGUST 7, 1864

Major-General SHERMAN, Commanding:

The bridge at Roswell has been destroyed and the regiment reported here. The commanding officer informs me that yesterday afternoon he saw clouds of dust some distance to the left, on the opposite side of the river, as of troops moving in that direction. Have you met any cavalry around your left?

J. McARTHUR
Brigadier-General156

Sherman sent General McArthur a reply to his question and made sure the General understood his feelings on protecting the army's rear.

HDQRS. Military Division of the
Mississippi, In the Field, near
Atlanta, August 7, 1864.

General McARTHUR:

Your dispatch received. General Garrard's cavalry on your left flank frequently patrols up as far as McAfee's Bridge above Roswell. The dust may have been his cavalry. Still I know the enemy will attempt by his cavalry to strike our road, and I want you to keep all on the lookout, and to fight like the devil. If any part allows itself to be surprised or defeated, he (the commander) had better drown himself.

W.T. SHERMAN
Major-General Commanding.157

In Louisville, Kentucky, an inspection of a newly built army hospital gives a clue to where the Roswell mill workers are confined.

LOUISVILLE, KY., August 7, 1864

Col. W. HOFFMAN, U.S. Army
Commissary-General of Prisoners
Washington, D.C.:

Colonel:...Several thousand dollars were expended last month in building a hospital, which is now completed. Upon being supplied with water and gas it can be used. I would recommend that the order be given for supplying the hospital with water and gas, as the building is now used by refugees, and will soon become in a very dirty condition...

C.T. ALEXANDER
Surgeon, U.S. Army.158

An interview with Mrs. Mildred Hill, of Woodstock, Georgia, whose grandmother was 12 years old when she and her family were sent north from Roswell by Federal troops, is consistent with Surgeon Alexander's report. Mrs. Hill's grandmother, her 16 year old sister, and their father,

..ended up in detention, in a cavernous stench-filled building in Louisville. The father begged the Union troops to let him and his daughters go into town to find work. He feared they would die of disease if they stayed where they were. Given permission, the girls found work, supporting their ailing father until they could return to Roswell.159

Colonel Eli Long (U.S.)
National Archives

Monday, August 8

Col. E. Long, commander of the 2nd Brigade, 2nd Cavalry Division. sent in his report of a patrol he sent to McAfee's Bridge.

> HDQRS. Second Brigade, Second
> Cavalry Division, Buckhead, Ga.,
> August 8, 1864.

Capt. ROBERT P. KENNEDY
Assistant Adjutant-General
Second Cavalry Division:

Captain: I have the honor to report, for the information of the Brigadier-General commanding, that I sent a scouting party of one battalion to McAfee's Bridge at an early hour this morning. Lieutenant-Colonel Pattern, First Ohio Cavalry, was in charge of this party, and has returned with his command. He reports having found no force of rebel cavalry in that neighborhood, nor could he hear of anything more than small squads. He saw but one or two stragglers of General Stoneman's command. He lost one horse killed, by being fired upon by a squad of men who escaped in the woods. From the best information he could gather he deemed it useless to remain longer, and returned to camp this evening.

I am, very respectfully, your obedient servant,

> ELI LONG
> Colonel, Commanding Brigade.160

Tuesday, August 9

The *Louisville Daily Journal* printed an article which they believed to be a fair explanation for General Sherman's actions towards the mill workers. The article is as follows:

The New York Commercial and other Eastern papers animadvert very severely upon General Sherman for sending the four hundred factory girls, taken at Rossville, (sic) to the North. This censure arises from a misapprehension of the facts, for the unfortunate operatives, thrown out of employment by the chances of war in an impoverished country, where everything had been taken for the support of the rebel army, and unable to obtain food, importuned

General Sherman to send them where they could find work and security. One of our correspondents described the scene as pitiable when the poor creatures clung to our officers, and in anguished tones begged to be removed from the scenes of desolation which everywhere surrounded them, and where, if they remained, nothing but starvation could be expected. In the exercise of an enlarged and generous spirit of humanity, the General acceded to their request.161

The latter part of the above explanation is questionable; as the factory workers at Roswell were charged with treason and sent north, whether they wanted to go or not. To shed some light on Sherman's true reason for charging the mill workers with treason, one must look at General Order No. 100, issued by the War Department, Adj. General's Office, in Washington D.C., on April 24, 1863. This order was titled *Instructions for the Government of Armies of the United States in the Field,* Section 10, Paragraph No. 157 states:

Armed or unarmed resistance by citizens of the United States against the lawful movements of their troops is levying war against the United States and is therefore treason.162

With this in mind, reread Sherman's orders to General Garrard, concerning the mill workers, on July 7, 1864, and Sherman's letter to General Halleck, in Washington, D.C., on July 9, 1864. Also, remember that the employees of the woolen mill refused to leave the building when ordered to do so, on July 6, 1864.

Wednesday, August 10

With so many people arriving from Georgia, the prison hospital in Louisville, Kentucky, was becoming full. A new location was obtained to handle the overcrowding. The following article is from the *Louisville Daily Journal*:

Female Military Prison-We understand that one of the houses on Broadway, between Twelfth and Thirteenth Streets, has been taken by the military authorities and transformed into a military prison, to be devoted exclusively to the confinement of females. A large number of such prisoners are already in the city, and they are daily received from Georgia, Tennessee, and Kentucky.163

Back in Marietta, Georgia, William King writes,

I hear orders have been sent to burn the Bridge at Roswell, which had been rebuilt by the Federal army, as they needed the bridge no longer. I fear their forces are to be withdrawn from Roswell, and that Brother Pratt and family will be exposed to the ravages of the bands of robbers pouring over the country. Lawlessness pervades the land. O this War!164

Author's Note: From this point on, there will be dates missing due to a lack of information for a day to day account of events.

Saturday, August 13

A proportion of Wheeler's Cavalry, C.S.A., had cut the railroad near Acworth. This inflamed Sherman, as seen in his order to General McArthur.

HDQRS. Military Division of the Mississippi, In the Field, near Atlanta, August 13, 1864.

General McARTHUR,
Marietta:

Make somebody suffer for the break of the railroad at Acworth; somebody over in the direction of Roswell or McAfee's Bridge. It would be well to keep a good picket out in that direction. The Macon papers announce the capture of Marietta by their cavalry. That indicates a purpose. I think you had better bring the Kennesaw force close in, with a regiment to picket the mountain, with a signal station.

W.T. SHERMAN,
Major-General, Commanding.165

Research has failed to show that any retaliation was taken against anyone in Roswell or at McAfee's Bridge, even though orders were issued to do so. However, Garrard's Cavalry was sent out to find the force responsible.

Sunday, August 14

HDQRS. Military Division of the
Mississippi, In the Field, near
Atlanta, August 14, 1864.

General Thomas:

General McArthur, at Marietta, reports small bodies of cavalry approach Marietta from the northeast. General Garrard should send frequently up to Roswell and McAfee's. You may order General Kilpatrick to lay down a bridge at Sandtown and be prepared to scour the country down as far as Camp Creek.

W.T. Sherman
Major-General Commanding.[166]

General Thomas was already on top of the problem, as seen in his reply back to Sherman.

Headquarters Department of the
Cumberland, August 14, 1864

Major-General SHERMAN:

Garrard has already received orders to scout as far as Roswell. He sent a scouting party some distance beyond Decatur, both south and in the direction of Covington, yesterday, but discovered nothing. Have sent orders for Kilpatrick to put down the bridge at Sandtown.

GEO. H. THOMAS,
Major-General.[167]

Thursday, August 18

Sherman has sent General Kilpatrick on a raid south of Atlanta and at the same time felt uneasy about the Confederate right flank, east of Atlanta. So again, the Federal high command looked toward Roswell as an important area.

SHERMAN'S HEADQUARTERS
August 18, 1864

General THOMAS:

Let General Garrard look well around Decatur to see if enemy's infantry is moving outside fortification of Atlanta in direction of Roswell.

W.T. SHERMAN,
Major-General.168

Saturday, August 20

Captain James R. King, commander of the Roswell Battalion appears on Confederate reports to have been captured by the 1st Brig. 2nd Cavalry Division, at Macon, Georgia. Captain A.A. Zachry takes charge of the battalion.

In Louisville, Kentucky, Provost Marshal Captain Jones is trying to find a way to disburse from his city, the hundreds of Southerners General Sherman has sent to the place. The *Louisville Daily Journal* printed the following:

About ten days ago, Captain Jones, Commissary General for rebel prisoners in the State of Kentucky, addressed a communication to General Sherman, stating that the large number of refugees and paroled prisoners sent north of the Ohio river to remain during the war, was inflicting serious injury upon the border of Indiana and especially on the city of Jeffersonville, and that the evil was felt by the prisoners released in the same proportion that the injury resulted to the Indiana borders. Under existing orders, the only course left open for him to pursue was to release all prisoners on the north bank of the Ohio River. He was not authorized to furnish them transportation to the interior portion of the state, and consequently a large number were left without employment or any means by which they could gain a support, as the applicants for employment were largely in excess of the demand for labor. A majority of the persons released north of the river were in destitute circumstances, and unable to pay their passage by rail or steamboat to points where honest employment might be obtained. The evil was a serious one, because the large number of persons left in idleness and want was calculated to develop crime. Driven to desperation by destitution, the deserters from the rebel army were

117

sorely tempted to violate the sacred obligation given to the United States Government. In conclusion, the Captain thought that the evil might be remedied by authorizing him to furnish those transportation on the account of the Government, to interior points where employment might be obtained. In reply to his letter, he received, by telegraph, General Order No. 22, from Headquarters, Department of this city. The order says;

1. Persons from the rebel army required by standing orders to be sent north of the Ohio river and discharged, as well as refugees, male and female, escaping from the dangers of civil war at the south, will on arrival at Cairo or Louisville, be forwarded, at the expense of the United States, if unable to pay their own way, to Cincinnatti or St. Louis by water, or to any point over one hundred miles by railroad.

2. Commanding officers at Cairo and Louisville with through agents of the Christian Commission or Labor agencies, will endeavor to put this class of people in the way of honest employment as much as possible.

by Command of Maj. Gen. Sherman.

By examining the wording of the order, it will readily be discovered that the clause 'over one hundred miles,' &c., is somewhat ambiguous. In transmitting it by telegraph, Capt. Jones is under the impression that the word not, which would give another complexion to the sentence, was omitted by the operators. However, he has to act upon the order as received, and the only construction that can be placed upon it with the absence of the negative, is, that the General intended that persons seeking employment not more than a hundred miles from the river, are abundantly able to travel the distance on foot. Those desiring to go farther will be furnished transportation. We cannot accept this construction, drawn from the actual wording of the order, as the true meaning of the same. We feel certain that the word **not** has been omitted. It is not necessary for us to argue, that, with the insertion of the negative, the order is more explicit, easier understood, and better calculated to accomplish good. To place the limit to be travelled on foot at one hundred miles would have about the same effect if the ratio was increased tenfold. The preparations for a journey of one hundred miles are about the same as they are for one thousand. If the paroled prisoners and refugees must travel one hundred miles in search of employment, we fear that but few of them will arouse themselves to the undertaking.169

Monday, August 22

William King is concerned for the safety of his friends in Roswell. He writes:

He could give me (through D. Young) no information on Bro. B. nor any other friends. Mr. Y had stopped at Bro. Pratt's at Roswell, & said all were well. Mr.

F. says he thinks the Federal troops had abandoned Roswell, & that it was now in possession of the Conf'ts, & that the Federal Army was concentrating more to the right of Atlanta & advancing Southward.170 [Mr. F. is Mr. Fletcher.]

Tuesday, August 23

Sherman still had his mind on Roswell, as seen in this order to General Thomas.

> HDQRS. Military Division of the
> Mississippi, In the Field, near
> Atlanta, August 23, 1864-7:30 P.M.
>
> General THOMAS:
>
> Have your signal corps provided with rockets, and agree upon signals by rockets or signal smoke for a few simple messages such as *all well, send boats to Campbellton, send a brigade, division, or regiment to Campbellton,* also *lookout for us at Roswell.* These signals may be of use to us when we get beyond safe distance for couriers via Sandtown.
>
> W.T. SHERMAN
> Major-General, Commanding.171

In Louisville, a reporter for the *Louisville Daily Journal* wants to inform his readers how the newspaper receives its facts for a story. The Roswell incident has been a newsworthy story for some time now, so he travels about the city to locate one of the mill hands, for an interview. The reporter wrote the following:

> I make inquires and fail a number of times to be any the wiser for my inquisitive labors. But I persevere. Riding by n(unreadable) suburbs of the town I see a young lady sitting on a chair on the piazza. I am impressed that I receive all needed knowledge from the lady if I can only muster enough of courage to introduce myself. But I am bashful—my cheeks crimson with blushes roseate, the sun's tint on evenings pale face; I hesitate suddenly, I recover my equanimity, and advance 'smiling like a basket of chips.' (Pardon this smile or metaphor as you please to call it.) Bowing in a style thoroughly Parisian, I support this with an innocent look, and then comes the 'Good Evening,' or 'Good day, Madam,' as the hour of the day would suggest. I am offered a chair and in less than five minutes we are conversing as socially and cozy as you please. Then comes the categories and inquires—all of which are

answered with an evident satisfaction to both parties. As a result of this mode of what might be called itemizing strategy, I give you the following: My fair informant, who was seven years as operative in one of the Rossville—or more properly Roswell—manufactories, says that the usual number of working hours were from twelve to fourteen.

Spinners made $27 per month, and paid $25 per month for board, leaving two dollars to purchase clothing, pay incidental expenses etc.

Weavers made from $50 to $100 per month, and paid $32 per month for board.

Reelers and carders made $47 per month—seven of which per week went for board.

Pressers, spinning hands, and carders were paid at the rate of $32, out of which there was little remaining after the poor girls paid their board.

The others did piece work. Receiving Confederate scrip in pay, I do not think it was a profitable working in the Roswell mills as it would have been in the Lowell factories. Massachusetts beats Georgia in this respect—both they equally strong of the nigger. There were about five hundred women operatives at Roswell, and some two hundred men—many of whom were detailed by the rebel authorities—such as consumptive and convalescents. The mills worked for two days and a half after the capture of the town, the hands believing the 'Yankee Government' was going to continue the manufacturing of cloth, sheeting, and so on. But they were disappointed. On the afternoon of the third day the three establishments received the torch, and lit the heavens with glare of configuration. The operatives looked on, some weeping and crying, while others laughed with joy. Such is life; such is human nature. The chief 'loss' of the largest mill was a Yankee, who has married a Georgia Lady. Most of the women employed there have been sent north, but many yet remain. Those at this post and about are ensnaring many of the blue coats, and between Justices of the Peace, army chaplains, and cupid, that gay and festive old man hymen is having some glorious fun.172

Wednesday, August 24

The 14th Ill. Infantry, Company D., marched from Acworth, Georgia, to Roswell and went into camp.

William King, in Marietta, makes an interesting note in his diary today concerning a former Roswell Mill worker.

While out this morning among the pickets I found a young Fed'l Sergeant named Green, who told me that he had worked 1 1/2 years at the Roswell factory, 2 years in Atlanta & has been 2 years in his Uncle (A. Green's) store in Marietta, & he knew me, that he had removed back to the north about

5 years ago, he seemed to be a sensible young man & promised to come & see me, while his picket station was so near to me.173

Meanwhile, in Louisville, Kentucky, the local citizens were becoming very concerned with the welfare of the refugees from Georgia. The concern focused on overcrowding at the two prison locations, the lack of shelter for the ones who had been released, proper food, and medical attention. The *Louisville Daily Journal* printed the following:

Aid for Refugees—We can add nothing to the elegance of the simple subjoined statement of the distress, destitution, and suffering which have befallen the unfortunate refugees from Southern homes, who have been exiled by the ruthless conscription of the rebels, or compelled to leave to save their lives. Their condition appeals strongly to the humanity, and liberality of our citizens, and we trust that the call of the Commission will meet a prompt response.

The Commission for the aid of refugees desire to call the earnest attention of the citizens to the following important facts: The number of refugees now in the city and vicinity, who need our attention, is over one thousand—and more are constantly coming up from the front. By a recent order of Gen. Sherman, there need be no further increase of these people at this point, and even those now here can be sent by Government transportation to other points north. At present there are nearly two hundred at the Refugee House on the corner of Broadway and Tenth street, and about one hundred more at the one on Broadway and Seventeeth. Many more are scattered in the woods around New Albany, Jeffersonville, and our own city. It is needless to dwell upon temptations, to which these latter unfortunates are exposed. Many of this class support themselves for the present by their own labor; but, as the season advances, the winter will find most of them poorly protected from its storms and snows, and they will all flock instinctively into the city for help. It is our duty to provide for these now, and, by a little timely aid, prevent an accumulation of evils that will close in the winter months be ten times more difficult to remove. Efforts are being made to provide houses for these refugees in distant parts of the country. In the meantime, the condition of the sick and destitute among them is deplorable in the extreme. They are in immediate need of proper food, medical attention, and care. A few noble-hearted ladies of the city have been doing what they could from day to day, and the surgeon of the prison, Dr. Brown, has visited them as constantly as his other duties would permit. There are children of every age, some so attenuated as to be living skeletons, perishing for want of proper care. Men, women, and children, of whom a vast majority are women and children, all lie together—dozens of families—in one room, and many utterly destitute. The government issues army rations to soldiers families alone, and all others must depend upon the benevolent among us for aid.

The Commission would therefore appeal in the strongest terms to the Christian charity and careful forethought of our citizens—in appeal which has never been made in vain—for funds whereby the sick and needy may receive proper care and support; but more especially whereby these refugees may all be collected for transportation to other points, where they can obtain permanent employment.

The following gentleman have been appointed to solicit contributions, and they will at once enter upon the work:

Messrs. John F. Jefferson, and W. Smith, (of Clark & Smith), for the district east of First street.

Messrs. R.J. Menefee and W.H. Walker from First to Third streets.

Messrs. E.B. Dupont and E.N. Maxwell from Third to Fifth streets.

Messrs. J.B. Torbitt and T.B. Overton from Fifth to Seventh streets.

Messrs. Geo. Ainslie and Geo. Meadows, west of Seventh street.174

[Surgeon Brown is Dr. E.O. Brown of the 26th Kentucky Inf. The 26th Kentucky Inf. was on guard duty at the military prisons in Louisville during this time.]

Thursday, August 25

The 14th Ill. Infantry, Company D which has been camped in Roswell, left for Marietta.

Friday, August 26

The 14th Ill. Infantry, Company B, went on a scouting mission from Acworth, Georgia to Lebanon, through Roswell, and on to Marietta. [Lebanon, Ga., was at the present location of where Old Holcomb Bridge Road crosses Vickery's Creek.]

The scouts reported Confederate troops at Roswell to Headquarters, who in turn quickly informed Col. Minty to be on guard against this new threat.

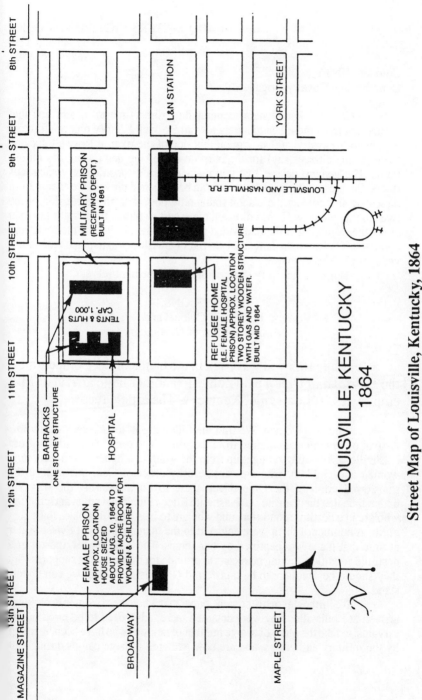

8th STREET
9th STREET
10th STREET
11th STREET
12th STREET
13th STREET
MAGAZINE STREET

L&N STATION

YORK STREET

LOUISVILLE AND NASHVILLE R.R.

MILITARY PRISON
(RECEIVING DEPOT)
BUILT IN 1861

REFUGEE HOME
(I.E. FEMALE HOSPITAL
PRISON) APPROX. LOCATION
TWO STOREY WOODEN STRUCTURE
WITH GAS AND WATER.
BUILT MID 1864

TENTS & HUTS
CAP. 1,000

BARRACKS
ONE STOREY STRUCTURE

HOSPITAL

FEMALE PRISON
(APPROX. LOCATION)
HOUSE SEIZED
ABOUT AUG. 10, 1864 TO
PROVIDE MORE ROOM FOR
WOMEN & CHILDREN

BROADWAY

MAPLE STREET

N

LOUISVILLE, KENTUCKY
1864

Street Map of Louisville, Kentucky, 1864
Map by Charles Brown

123

HEADQUARTERS TWENTIETH CORPS,
Near Atlanta, Ga.,
August 26, 1864

Colonel MINTY,
Commanding Cavalry Brigade:

Colonel: The General commanding directs me to inform you that scouts sent from these headquarters toward Roswell Factory report a force of the enemy's cavalry, 400 strong, on this side of the river at Roswell, located there (as the citizens say) for the purpose of making demonstrations on our trains. The general desires that you make such a disposition of your troops (those that are to remain up the river from here) as will prevent the enemy from molesting in any way the wagon trains now posted on the north side of the river in this vicinity. He has directed his escort to picket for tonight the road along the railroad and the one which passes by signal hill. All the roads and approaches between the latter and the river he wishes you to place guards and vedettes on. Please answer.

I am, Colonel, very respectfully, your obedient servant,

H.W. PERKINS,
Lieutenant-Colonel and
Assistant Adjutant-General.175

While Roswell was back in the hands of the Confederates, the *Patriot and Union* paid notice to another large arrival of Mill employees, at Louisville, Kentucky. The article reads:

Raids on Women. We find the following in the *Louisville Journal:* Arrival of women and children from the south. The train which arrived from Nashville last evening brought up from the south two hundred and forty nine women and children, who are sent here by order of Gen. Sherman, to be transferred north of the Ohio River, there to remain during the war. We understand that there are now at Nashville fifteen hundred women and children who are in a destitute condition, and who are to be sent to this place to be sent north. A number of them were engaged in the manufactories at Sweet-Water at time that place was captured by our forces. These people are mostly in a destitute condition, having no means to provide for themselves a support. Why they should be sent here to be transferred North is more than we can understand.

We further learn by the same paper that when these women & children arrived at Louisville, they were detained there, advertised to be hired out as servants, to take the place of a large number of negroes who have been liberated by the military authorities, and are now gathered in large camps throughout

124

Kentucky, where they are fed and supported in idleness and viciousness at the expense of the loyal taxpayers.

Thus while these negro women are rioting and luxuriating in the Federal camps on the bounty of the Government the white women and children of the south are arrested at their homes and sent off as prisoners to a distant country, to be sold into bondage, as the following advertisement fully attests:

NOTICE—Families residing in the city or country wishing seamstress or servants can be suited by applying at the refugee quarters on Broadway, between Ninth and Tenth. This is sanctioned by Capt. Jones, Provost Marshall.—Constitution Union.176

Saturday, August 27

Travel in and out of Roswell and Marietta was impossible, due to Confederate activity in these areas. William King writes:

I am at a loss what to do, I cannot remain much longer, and to leave the house unprotected will secure its destruction. I had hoped to get Mr. Rowland & family from Roswell to occupy it, they are anxious to do, but as his work is in town the prohibition of passing in & out of town renders it impossible to do so, and no suitable person can be got unless we will feed them, as they can get no work out of town.177

Sunday, August 28

Confederate cavalry are holding Roswell and are using it as their base of operations, as this next Federal report describes:

HEADQUARTERS TWENTIETH CORPS,
Chattahoochee River,
August 28, 1864

Lieut. M.J. KELLY,
Chief of Couriers:

Lieutenant: ...Colonel Minty has one regiment of cavalry up the river from here toward Roswell Factory and two regiments at Sandtown. The enemy's cavalry hold Roswell. Their force there is supposed to be about 400. They scout down the river as far as Soap Creek.

Yours respectfully,

H.W. PERKINS,
Assistant Adjutant-
General.[178]

Tuesday, August 30

In General Garrard's daily report, he states one regiment of Minty's Cavalry is still patrolling the area east of Roswell.

Wednesday, August 31

The first day of the battle of Jonesboro is fought, south of Atlanta, and ends in a Confederate defeat.

September 1864

Thursday, September 1

The second day of the battle of Jonesboro ends in another defeat for the Confederates.

Meanwhile, in Marietta, Ga., William King makes note of an incident which involves the Confederate Cavalry at Roswell.

I heard in town that Smith, one of the Ros'l Factory Wagoners, had been hung by our scouts at Roswell for becoming a Union man, I cannot however believe the report, if he is hung at all I am sure it must be from desertion.... I learn that it is too unsafe for anyone to try to go over to Roswell, even with a government pass, from scouts, deserters & bush whackers on the way.[179]

To support Mr. King's conclusion of the hanging, is an article which appeared in the July 28, 1864 issue of the Southern Watchman, an Athens', Georgia newspaper.

...No deserter is allowed to remain in that section of the country occupied by Sherman, but is immediately sent North. The large number who have left Hood's Army have rightfully served. This fact should be widely circulated in Hood's army. ...There is another item akin to it. Those Confederates who remained and took the oath, while they are despised by the Yankees, receive no mercy from our scouts, who hang them whenever they can lay their hands on them.[180]

Friday, September 2

General Slocum telegraphs Washington to inform them Atlanta has fallen.

Atlanta, Ga., September 2, 1864.
(Received 10:05 p.m.)

Hon. E.M. STANTON,
Secretary of War:

General Sherman has taken Atlanta. The twentieth Corps occupies the city. The main army is on the Macon Road, near East Point. A battle was fought near that point, in which General Sherman was Successful. Particulars not known.

H.W. SLOCUM,
Major-General.181

With the fall of Atlanta, the Roswell Battalion, (presently at Monticello, Georgia), is assigned to Hannon's Brigade, of Wheeler's Cavalry. 182

Sunday, September 4

Sherman issues new orders for his army's placement around Atlanta, until a new campaign is planned. General Garrard is ordered to cover areas along the Chattahoochee River, of which one of the points is Roswell. Then orders were issued by Sherman's acting Assistant Adjutant General, to Garrard, informing him to cover the area south and east of Roswell.

HDQRS. Chief of Cavalry, Dept.
of the Cumberland, Camp near
Lovejoy's, September 4, 1864

Brig. Gen. K. GARRARD,
Commanding Second Division Cavalry:

...with you command, take post, headquarters at Cross Keys, picketing from Stone Mountain to the crossing of the Chattahoochee on the road from Pinckneyville to Warsaw....

I am, General, very respectfully, your obedient servant,
DAVID F. HOW,
Lieutenant and Acting
Assistant Adjutant-General.[183]

(The site of the town of Pinckneyville is at the modern intersection of North Peachtree Street and Spalding Drive. Crosskeys is at the modern intersection of Ashford Dunwoody Road, and South Johnson Ferry Road. Warsaw was in the area of the modern intersection of Old Alabama Road and Medlock Bridge Road.)

Friday, September 9

Attention is again given to the mill workers. This time the Editor from the *Louisville Journal* visits the people, while still in their confinement, in Louisville, Ky. the following article appeared in the New York Commercial Advertisers:

Sherman's Female Captives... It will be remembered that General Sherman on occupying Marietta and vicinity, sent several hundred of the females employed in the rebel factories North. Most of them tarried at Louisville, where they at present remain. On Saturday the Editor of the Louisville Journal paid them visit which he describes as follows: As we ascended the steps, the first object that greeted our eyes was a child full of robust health engaged at play in the hall. Passing through the lower apartments, the doors standing wide open, we found, on an average, three double beds, in each room, and, seated around and on the beds, engaged in sewing, and other occupations common to ladies, were women—some with the bloom of eighteen years upon their cheeks, and others advanced in years beyond the hey-day of life.

They greeted our entrance with marked politeness, addressing the Major, who visits the prison daily, in a manner free from restraint, and often with a smile. The rooms were clean and airy, though not furnished with that magnificence indicating opulence or independence. In every room, bare-headed, rosy-cheeked, dirty- faced children, full of the innocent prattle of childhood, were playing upon the floor, kicking up their heels in the most abandoned manner. The apartments on the second floor are not different from those on the first. The windows were raised, and the air, laden with the fragrance of fruit trees, swept softly through the casements. A few of the prisoners were dressed with marked tidiness, and spoke in cheerful tones. Their bearing was such to impress the stranger that they were reared in the hall of refinement. A majority were very careless in regard to dress, and their toilet was not calculated to make a favorable impression.

Some moved about the building in a sprightly manner, others with their robes gathered negligently about them, and with all the languor to be found in the invalid, or in the person prone to yield to gloomy thought, and grow sad and morose. They spoke with that freedom which in a sure index that nor restraint is placed upon their conversation. All had relatives or dear friends in the Confederate Army. That mother, with the laughing child upon her knee, recalled the sunny home in the far-away land, and was proud that the husband and father was a soldier in the rebel army. This matron in the neat white cap, concealing the silver threads of age, had pressed the parting kiss upon her darling boy's brow—the hope of her declining years—and bid him ever to be true to the tri-barred flag. This young girl, full of the freshness of youth, had whispered love and parting beneat'n the starlight sky, and now she glorified that her lover was a war- torn veteran in defense of the confederate cause.

For an hour we sat and listened to their conversation, closely marketing the accent and manner of expression; and, to speak with all respect due the captives, it is our candid opinion that but very few of the inmates of the prison would be recognized by an F.F.V. as an equal in refinement and social position. The prisoners, at least a majority of them, are not of the first families of the south. In two of the rooms in the back part of the building, a sad sight was presented to view. On the beds were stretched feeble forms, some with faces pale and wary, others with brows flushed with burning fever. One lady in the prime of life, was convalved with excruciating pain, and her faint moaning fell mostly upon the ear, telling how deeply she suffered.

On a low cot was stretched a fair-haired boy, pale, very pale, feeble and convalescent. A faint smile wreathed his lips as we bent over him, and kindly inquired how 'he felt today.' he answered, 'better, much better.' Aside from these passages, the prison was as cheerful as the most sanguine could expect. The grounds surrounding the house are spacious, and shaded with fruit and ornamental trees. The prisoners are allowed the full freedom of the grounds. Army rations are furnished, yet prepared in such a manner as to render them palatable even to the delicate. The authorities have proffered to release all the captors North of the Ohio River, but they say, that in accepting the conditions, they would be thrown penniless and alone in a land of utter strangers, and it is better that they should remain where they are. Colonel Farileigh and Major Magruder take the best possible care of the prisoners under the circumstances, and allow them every privilege consistent with their ideas of duty. The quarters are airy, comfortable, and healthy.184

(The Colonel is Lieut. Colonel Thomas B. Farileigh of the 26th Kentucky Infantry, U.S., and Post Commandant of Louisville. Major Magruder is believed to be Major Alexander Magruder of the 27th Kentucky Inf., U.S.)

At different periods of time, groups of the mill workers were released. A 1932 interview with S.H. Causey, a former 1864 mill employee from Sweet Water, stated he

and his family found employment in Indianapolis....185

Samuel Farr a Roswell mill worker, along with his wife, Jane Farr, and their two year old son, Jonathan Farr also found employment in Indianapolis, Indiana.

Sunday, September 18

Major Matthew J. Williams, a resident in Marietta, noted in his diary that not all of the Roswell mill workers made the trip north. Major Williams writes:

Two girls, both young and both formerly of Roswell factory, came in this afternoon for roses one of them was quite pretty & the other good looking. Both lacked the charm of retiring modesty. I plucked or cut roses for them.186

Thursday, September 22

It is not known when the Confederates left Roswell; but, it appears they are gone by now, as Federal troops are back in the area. The following is a report from Captain Greeno, who is camped near Roswell.

ON ROAD NEAR SANDTOWN BRIDGE,
September 22, 1864

(General KILPATRICK)

General: I left camp near Roswell yesterday morning with a detachment of the First Cavalry Brigade, Second Division, with orders to make a reconnaissance on this side of the river as far as Franklin if possible. I have 150 enlisted men and officers...

Very respectfully, your obedient servant,
C.L. GREENO,
Captain, Commanding Detachment
First Cavalry Brigade.187

Back in Louisville, Ky., the need for medical care was so great for the mill hands that a female doctor was assigned to them.

Assistant Surgeon Gen'ls Office
Louisville, Ky.
Sept. 22nd 1864

In accordance with instructions from Major General Sherman Commanding Military Division of Mississippi, Miss Mary E. Walker M.D. will report in person, without delay for duty with female prisoners in this city.

By Order of the Asst. Surgeon Gen'l
Joseph B. BROWN
Surgeon U.S. Army. 188

Dr. Mary Walker
U.S. Army Military History Institute

Friday, September 23

An appeal for help, for the confined mill employees, is again published in the local newspaper. Also, the number of persons detained has declined. The *Louisville Daily Journal* writes:

Sick Women and Children—The Refugee Commission have again to ask the aid of our citizens. During the past few weeks several hundred refugees have been provided for and sent from the city. Many yet remain, and there are now in the Refugee-house, on Broadway, over one hundred and fifty women and children, of whom nine-tenths are prostrate with disease. Several deaths have occurred during this week; the sickness has assumed a typhoid form, and the physician in charge says immediate relief must be given, or all will die. They must be removed to other quarters, what little they have now being rotten with filth and vermin. Arrangements are being made for their removal today; and, in order that they may leave behind them their dirt and rags, immediated contributions are needed of bedding and clothing, suitable for sick women and children. Will not our ladies give such articles as they can spare? No matter how few or common or how much worn, all will be most acceptable, and each one may save a life. To do the greatest good, what is given should be sent by 10 o'clock this morning to the stores of Messrs. Dow & Burkhardt, or John F. Jefferson, on, Market Street; and every lady who reads this notice is urged by the love she has for her own children to do what she can for these sick and dying ones.[189]

Monday, September 26

Union and southern forces clash again, just outside of Roswell. A detachment of the 4th Michigan Cavalry was attacked by a mounted Confederate command, immediately north of the town. The Adjutant General, for the state of Michigan, made the following report of the incident:

Lieutenant Boutelle, of Company B, with a detail of 50 men sent out as guard to a forage train, were attacked by a force estimated at 200 mounted men. Boutelle drew sabres and charged, driving the rebels off, but he received a ball through his right hand, the bones of which were badly shattered, while two of his men were captured. On their way back to camp they were again attacked by the same rebel force, and again the gallant Boutelle led a successful charge against them, his useless right hand hanging by his side.[190]

Wednesday, September 28

General Elliott, who is in charge of Sherman's Cavalry, orders most of General Garrard's Cavalry to the west of Atlanta, but makes sure the northeastern area of the city is covered.

Atlanta, September 28, 1864

General GARRARD,
Commanding Second Division Cavalry:

Detail one regiment for picket at Blake's Mill and another for Roswell. Concentrate the remainder of your division, with battery, on right bank of the Chattahoochee, near railroad bridge or Sweet Water town—preferably at the latter point—and be prepared for a rapid movement of five or six days. Keep me informed of your position, so that I may join you when you reach the point designated. This move should be made as soon as possible.

W.T.ELLIOTT
Brigadier-General.,
Chief of Cavalry.191

(Blake's Mill was located near Shallowford Road, where it crosses Peachtree Creek, 2/10 of a mile east of I-85.)

About this time, James M. Drake, of the Roswell Troopers, (Company E, Cobb's Legion) was in Newtown, Georgia, after obtaining permission to go home to get a horse. Due to the Federal Cavalry patrols in the area, Pvt. Drake could not return to his command in Virginia. Like other Confederate soldiers on furlough and cut off from returning to their commands, Pvt. Drake was ordered to report to Confederate General Wofford's command at Cumming, Georgia. (Newtown, Ga., was located about 4 miles northeast of Roswell.)

**Private James M. Drake of the
Roswell Troopers**
Courtesy of Eleanor Drake

Thursday, September 29

Major Jennings in command of the first Brigade, of the Second U.S. Cavalry division, camped just west of Roswell, wrote a report concerning confederate activity north of Roswell.

HDQRS. FIRST BRIGADE, SECOND
CAVALRY DIVISION,
Between Marietta and Roswell,
September 29, 1864

Capt. LEVI T. GRIFFIN,
Acting Assistant Adjutant-General:

Captain: Since our arrival here yesterday morning nothing of importance has occurred. One of the men of the fourth Michigan Cavalry, who was captured on the 25th[**] instant, escaped on the next day and has returned to the command. He reports having been carried that night to Cumming, via Alpharetta. On the way he passed through different squads of the rebels in tens, twenties, and fifties, numbering in all at least 1,000. He appears quite positive to their numbers. In one camp they had 200, probably the same party which attacked our forage train the next day. The most of them were dressed in our uniforms. he was taken before Colonel Hill, Sixth Texas Cavalry (Thirty- fifth Tennessee Infantry), who has his headquarters about five miles this side of Cumming, and there closely questioned. Colonel Hill, who commands the forces there, appeared to be well acquainted with our numbers and position. Citizens report that a part of the force was to move toward Dalton on Tuesday. I have forwarded to General Elliot's headquarters and to Captain McBurney all reports due to this date.

Very respectfully yours,
W.H. JENNINGS,

Major, Commanding First Brigade.[192]

[**]The 25th is the wrong date, this incident actually occurred on September 26, 1864.

October 1864

Saturday, October 1

Major Jennings moves out of the Roswell area, with his brigade, in compliance with the orders issued on September 28. There are no longer any Federal Troops camped in Roswell; however, the 9th Michigan Cavalry, which is camped at Decatur, Ga., patrols the roads from that location to Roswell.

Monday, October 3

Back in Louisville, Ky., Federal General Schofield, un-covers widespread corruption involving the military police at that location. It is not known if the mill workers were caught up in this situation, but there is a good chance some probably were, as some were still confined in Louisville. General Schofield reported his findings to General Sherman in Atlanta.

Louisville, Ky.,
October 3, 1864

Maj. Gen. W.T. SHERMAN,
Commanding Military Division of the Mississippi:

General: during my brief visit to Kentucky I have learned that affairs here are in some respects in a very bad condition. There seemed to have been criminal looseness, and in some instances, gross corruption in the administration of military justice. Public enemies of the worst character have received their liberty by payment of large fees to lawyers having personal influence with commanding officers, while innocent persons have been kept in prison a long time without trial. The provost-marshal's department at Louisville and the military police in the District of Kentucky appear to have been mainly engaged in trading Negro substitutes and extorting fines for violation of petty regulations. The officers of police appear to have performed all the duties of public prosecutors, judge, and receiver of moneys. These seem to be notorious facts. An investigation into the transactions of the police and provost marshals is now progressing, and I have ordered the arrest of the parties so far implicated. The charges relative to corruption in the release of prisoners involve the official character of Brevet-Major-General Burbridge, who is now absent and has been acting in reference to the arrest and disposition of disloyal persons under direct orders from your headquarters. Because of these facts I have taken no steps to investigate the charges which may affect General Burbridge, and respectfully refer the matter to you for such action as you may deem proper.

I am, General very respectfully, your obedient servant,

J.M. SCHOFIELD,
Major-General. 193

To support the theory that some, or a good many of the mill workers may have been caught up in this situation, look back to the August 25, *Patriot and Union* article concerning the mill employees.

General Burbridge was relieved from his command in the District of Kentucky in January of 1865, and on October 16, 1865, he wrote the following in his defense:

I am surrounded by petty annoyances that individually I have no power to remove. Three officers of my command have been the means of injuring me personally, and the cause generally, by their acts and assertions, for which the public hold me responsible. I have reference to Capt. H.B. Grant, twenty- seventh Kentucky Infantry, Inspector-General of the district; Capt. Steph. Jones, aide-de-camp and commissary-general of prisoners for this district, and Lieut. Col. J.H. Hammond, assistant adjutent-general, in charge of the camp of the draft rendezvous. Captain Grant was appointed by General Schofield and Captain Jones by the Secretary of War; they are both rabid McClellan men, and are using their influence and position against me, in my endeavor to carry the state for Mr. Lincoln.194

Major-General J.M. Schofield (U.S.)
Battles and Leaders of the Civil War, 1956

Monday, October 24

The 9th Michigan Cavalry is having a hard time patroling east of Roswell; because there has been so much military activity in the area that once-plentiful forage has almost all but disappeared. This is greatly affecting their horses. A report by Company D of the 9th Michigan Cavalry states:

What little forage our horses have had for the last month has been obtained from the country, in many cases it could only be procured at a distance of miles from camp. These severe marches together with the heavy loads the horses have had to carry have rendered many of them unservicable. A portion of the command is dismounted.195

However, this does not keep the 9th Mich. Cav. from patroling as far as Roswell. Five members of the Roswell Battalion are captured in Roswell, by Lt. Col. Wm. B. Way.

The captured men are: Sgt. C.W. Faulkner, Sgt. Raford J. Groover, Sgt. Raybond Groover, 2nd lt. Frank J. Minhinnett, and Pvt. Luther Sherman. There men are sent to the military prison in Louisville, Ky., and from there to Camp Douglas, Ill. except 2nd Lt. Minhinnett. He is sent to Johnson Island prison, Ohio, because of his rank.

Back at Roswell, Capt. D.W. Sedwick, commanding a detachment of the 102nd Illinois Infantry had better luck with obtaining forage in the area. He reported the expedition,

Returned with thirty-seven loads of forage and three wagon loads of potatoes.196

Lieutenant Colonel William B. Way
(U.S.)
U.S. Army Military History Institute

Camp Douglas, Illinois
National Archives

November 1864

Friday, November 11

Gen. Sherman telegraphs Maj. General Halleck, in Washington, D.C. that there is no longer a need to hold Atlanta. The message states:

...Atlanta itself is only of strategic value as long as it is a railroad center; and as all the railroads leading to it are destroyed, as well as all its foundries, machine-shops, ware-houses, depots, &c., it is of no more value than any other point in North Georgia:...197

Saturday, November 12

At 2:25 p.m., Sherman sends his last dispatch from Atlanta before severing communications. Sherman then begins his *March to the Sea,* and Federal troops cease to visit Roswell.

December 1864

Thursday, December 15

Rev. N.A. Pratt writes his nephew,Confederate Col. Barrington S. King, of the new trouble in Roswell: Confederate Army deserters. Rev. Pratt writes:

...Our greatest trouble now arises from soldiers at home without leave—we have here in the neighborhood it is said from 40 to 50 soldiers, some of whom are stealing horses & mules, taking the few hogs left from the already robbed & almost starving soldiers wives & poor widows. Those here resist the laws of the council swearing they will cut trees in the streets, burn rails & planks wherever they find them. Is there no way of getting such fellows back to their commands? They are a nuisance, those I know here are Henry, Cobb, Smith, Riding, Owen the latter is sick George, Roberts, and many others who have been two three and five months.198

(Of the names Rev. Pratt writes that he knew, five are unreadable, so are not written in the copy of the letter.)

January 1865

Sunday, January 1

Of the five men captured in Roswell on Oct. 24, two of them write a letter, to the Federal authorities at the Camp Douglas Military Prison, claiming that they had deserted the rebel army in order to take advantage of the Amnesty Proclamation. These two men are Sgt. C.W. Faulkner and Sgt. Raford J. Groover. Both letters are almost word for word the same, so only Sgt. Faulkner's will be printed here.

CAMP DOUGLAS, CHICAGO, ILLS.
January 1, 1865

Sir,

I, C.W. Faulkner, a private of Co. A. Ross. Battery, would respectfully represent that I was conscripted into the rebel service at Roswell, Georgia on the 24th Oct., 1862 and forced to bear arms against the Government of the United States against my will and consent, as I have always maintained the principles of a true and loyal Union man.

I would further represent that I deserted the Rebel service at Roswell, Georgia on Oct. 1864 and voluntarily surrendered myself to the 9th Michigan Cavalry to avail myself of the Amnesty Proclamation, and that I do not desire to be returned South in exchange; but would respectfully ask that permission be granted to me to take the Oath of Allegiance to the United States, and again enjoy the privileges of an American Citizen. I am Sir

Very Respectfully,
C.W. FAULKNER
Co. A. Roswell Battery
Artillery.199

There are several falsehoods in this letter. C.W. Faulkner was a Sergeant in the Roswell Battalion at the time of his capture, not a private as he writes; also, before becoming a Sgt. he was a lieutenant. Why he was demoted, on June 2, 1864, is not known. By Confederate war records, Sgt. Faulkner enlisted in the battalion on June 28th, 1863, for the duration of the war, not Oct. 24, 1862. The battalion did not exist until 1863. As far as not desiring to return South, C.W. Faulkner is buried in the Presbyterian cemetery in Roswell, next to Oak Street. He died in 1903. Sgt. Faulkner may have written what he did because he may have felt that if the Federal authorities knew he held a rank in the Confederate Army they would not release him from prison. The letter did not help for he was not released from prison until May 1, 1865.

Sunday, January 8

Pvt. Luther Sherman, one of the five men captured in Roswell, on Oct. 24, dies of chronic diarrhea. He was buried in grave 424, at Block 2 Chicago City Cemetery. In 1867, the Confederate dead in the City Cemetery were removed and interred in a mass, common grave at Oak Woods Cemetery in Chicago.

Sunday, January 15

In Louisville, a disturbance broke out at the female prison, also called the refugee house, because the mill hands did not like the way Dr. Mary Walker was treating them. The Commandant of Louisville in turn criticized the doctor. Angered because the

Commandant did not come to her defense, Dr. Walker wrote a letter to him justifying her actions.

Commandant of Post
Louisville, Ky.

You have done me a gross injustice in speaking of me as you do, when I appealed to you to sustain me in the right.

I thought you a man of sufficient discretion and judgement to comprehend things as they exist—, and then I thought you had sufficient moral courage to pursue a course consistent with an enlightened conscience.

The substance of the whole cause of disturbance can be summed up on the following—First, I would not allow rebel songs and disloyal talk. The Lieut. would say 'O they are women.' Second, I would not allow familiarity between the guards, male cooks and prisoners. Third, all four of the male cooks were relieved and females supplied in their places, by the direction of Col. Farleigh. Fourth, I exacted cleanliness. Fifth, I would not allow prisoners to abuse each other. Sixth, I would not allow them to neglect their small children, or abuse them. To explain—one woman when her babe was but 4 or 5 weeks old would put in a crib nights, and leave it until morning without any attention and it would cry until it was hoarse, and I finally took the crib out of the room and compelled her to take it into bed with her and take care of it. Another who has two children under 4 years, would allow them to cry and scream in the filth and wish them dead, until I told her if she did not pay them sanitary attention, I would have them given to someone who would. another was about to hang her niece with a rope to scare her into obedience when I condemned such proceedings not only but told her I would not allow it. The subject was the oldest of three orphaned children, whose father died in the rebel army and whose mother died here in prison about the first of Oct. 64.

Seventh, I watched their rebel friends when they came here and would not allow them to pass letters without examining them, and would not allow talk I did not hear.

Eighth, I had one woman handcuffed about two hours for calling the Guard to his face 'D.S.B.' and threatening to 'kill two other prisoners' and 'daring me to come up stairs.' I also had several locked up in the outside store house for waving their handkerchief and yelling for Jeff Davis when rebel prisoners were passing.

The food question is only a pretense and if Lieut. Stephenson had three grains of common sense he would see it. They complained every meal when there were four men cooks and I gave no direction whatever.

Give them their filth, unrestrained disloyalty and immorality and it will be satisfactory times with them. I am an eye sore to them, and they want men cooks again, and a man Doctor. They glory in a Lieut. that chops open doors and allows them to surround him in the operation. He would not have

146

dared made such an outright idiot of himself if Col. Fairleigh had been here. Col. Fairleigh has learned my true motives for all that I have done, and appreciates the trying position I hold, and all my greatest superior officers have confidence in my having done well under all circumstances, and that confidence is merited.

With due respect,
MARY E. WALKER U.S.A.[200]

February 1865

Sunday, February 18

In Washington D.C., Brig. Gen. Hoffman, Commissary-General of Prisoners had heard reports of female prisoners, in detention, in Louisville, Kentucky. he wrote Captain Jones about this matter.

OFFICE COMMISSARY-GENERAL OF PRISONERS,
Washington, D.C. February 18, 1865.

Capt. S.E. JONES, Provost-Marshal, Louisville, Ky.

Captain: I am directed by the Commissary-General of Prisoners to inquire if there is a female prison or hospital under your charge at Louisville district from the regular military prison and hospital, and to request, if such is the case, that you will report the number of prisoners confined there and the number of employees connected with it to this office.

Very respectfully, your obedient servant,

G. BLAGDEN,
Major, Second Mass. Cav.,
Asst. to Com. Gen. of Prisoners.[201]

Thursday, February 23

Captain Jones gives his reply to Washington, D.C. on the female prison question. His reply shows that most of the mill hands have been released. The few that remain may have been too sick to move.

147

Louisville, Ky.
February 23, 1865.

Respectfully return to Brig. Gen W. Hoffman, Commissary-General of Prisoners, with the information that there is no female prison of hospital under my charge, but that there is one at this place under command of the post commandant, organized under orders from Brevet Major-General Burbridge, commanding District of Kentucky. It is learned from the officer in immediate charge (whose reports are enclosed herewith) that there are 20 women and 14 children confined in it, and 1 doctress, 1 stewardess, and 1 orderly connected with the hospital department, and 1 commissioned officer, 2 non- commissioned officers, and from 7 to 10 privates acting as guards of the prison.

Stephen E. JONES
Captain and Additional Aide-de Camp.202
[The 1 doctress is Dr. Mary Walker and the 1 commissioned officer is Lieut. George Shane].

March 1865

Wednesday, March 22

Doctor Mary E. Walker is relieved from her duties in Louisville.

Assistant Surgeon General's Office
Louisville, Ky.
March 22nd, 1865

In conformity with the recommendation of the Medical Director of the Department of Kentucky, and the wishes of Mary E. Walker Actg. Asst. Surgeon U.S.A. for duty in the front, she is hereby relieved from duty in the Female Military Prison at Louisville, Ky...and will proceed without delay to Nashville, Tenn. and report in person for duty to Surgeon Geo. E. Cooper U.S.A. Medical Director of the Department of the Cumberland.
By order of the Asst. Surgeon General

JOSEPH B. BROWN
Surgeon U.S. Army.203

148

In May of 1865, Dr. Walker was still defending her actions at the female prison. The *Louisville Daily Journal* wrote an article which Dr. Walker took as *slander* towards her person. She wrote a rebuttal which the same newspaper printed.

Any little difficulties that may have occurred while on duty Louisville, Ky., were all that legitimately arose from a faithful performance of my duties under my orders and my oath to the United States, and not one moral loyalist with whom I have the honor of an acquaintance in Louisville can or will speak of me in other terms than those of commendation.

My position was one peculiarly trying, one which the post Commandant informed me upon my arrival, 'to have made him more trouble than all the other business combined.' To do my whole duty to the Government, and make the 'Prison' a place that was not a discredit to civilization, and keep it such, required my almost constant presence, and not until a short time before I left, did I fail to exclude myself almost entirely from society,...204

April 1865
Friday, April 21

The remaining women and children, still confined in Louisville, Ky. as of February 23, 1865 are believed to have gained their freedom as the following report states:

HEADQUARTERS MILITARY COMMANDER,
PROVOST MARSHALL'S OFFICE.

Louisvill, Ky, April 21, 1865.

Special Order
No. 48

[Extract]

. . . .

II. The following named female prisoners, now confined in the Female Military Prison, are unconditionally released from arrest and allowed to return to their homes.

By command of Brevet Brig.-Gen. L.D. WATKINS

Military Commander

Lieut. GEORGE SHANE, Superintendent.205

Wednesday, April 26

Confederate General J. Johnston, back in command of the remainder of his army, surrenders to Union General W.T. Sherman near Durham's Station, North Carolina.

May 1865

Saturday, May 20

The men left in the Roswell Battalion surrender themselves to Federal Authorities in Augusta, Georgia and then take the oath of allegiance.

June 1865

Wednesday, June 7

In a letter this date, from Atlanta, Barrington King writes that he will return to Roswell to rebuild.

...Expect to return in a few days for Roswell. It makes me sad to go there, but in my opinion best to try the old place, & if our state affairs are satisfactorily arranged, so as to protect life and property & make a support. I am getting old & anxious to do what may be in my power, to restore the comforts of old Roswell...[206]

Brigadier General D.C. McCallum
(U.S.)
National Archives

July 1865

Wednesday, July 19

At the Roswell Manufacturing Company's stock-holders meeting, the first since the war ended, Barrington King makes a statement concerning the mill workers on their actions on July 6, 1864.

We regret much to report the conduct of a few men, in our employment for years with the women and children, from whom we expected protection from our property—they plundered & destroyed to a large amount, tearing down the shelves in the store to burn, breaking glasses, and otherwise injuring the houses, hauling off iron and copper to sell and putting the wheel in motion and seriously injuring it by throwing down rocks.207

With the war over, most of the mill workers, charged with treason, returned home. Samuel Farr and his family returned to Roswell and they are buried in the Roswell Methodist Cemetery. Many others returned, according to S.H. Causey, a former Sweet Water Factory Employee:

Great was the rejoicing when the smoke of battle had cleared, and by the end of the summer of 1865 practically all of them rejoined their husbands, fathers and sweethearts in their former Roswell and Sweetwater homes. ...as soon as peace was declared they returned home, making the trip aboard the same train which had taken them north a year before.208

The main reason why the true number of Roswell Mill workers sent north or returned is not known, as well as their names, is given in this 1866 military report by Brevet Brigadier-General D.C. McCallum:

152

No record was kept of the contrabands, refugees, and rebels deserters that poured back of active operations. General Sherman ordered all sent to the rear who could not feed themselves, and they were placed upon the first train going in the direction by post commanders...209

Saturday, July 22

Barrington King writes a letter to his son Ralph King, explaining the present condition in Roswell:

...Everyone around seems to feel the loss sustained by destruction of the mills, and are anxious that we rebuild. Some of the families that were sent north have returned. The returned soldiers are anxious to work at 60 cents a day, and appear very orderly.210

☆☆☆☆

Roswell survived the destructive path of war, those who returned put the past behind them. The town grew larger after 1865, and to this day is still growing.

Thomas Hugh Kendley
Courtesy of George H. Kendley

Appendix A

Examples of the fate of some of the Roswell mill employees sent to the North

Mary Kendley- Sent to Louisville, Ky., then to Indianapolis, Ind., then to Cannelton, Ind. Married Albert May on July 19, 1865. They visited Roswell in the summer of 1873 and again in 1910. Mary Kendley May died April 21, 1924 in Cannelton, Ind.

Thomas Hugh Kendley- Sent to Louisville, Ky., then to Indianapolis, Ind., then to Cannelton, Ind. He worked in the Indiana Cotton Mills, Cannelton, Ind., died October 7, 1915. He is buried in Cannelton, and was 69 years old at the time of his death.

George Kendley- Sent to Louisville, Ky., then Indianapolis, Ind., then to Cannelton, Ind. Worked in the Indiana Cotton Mills in Cannelton for more than 50 years, married Lucetta Johnson.

Sara Jane Kendley- Sent to Louisville, Ky., then to Indianapolis, Ind., then to Cannelton, Ind. to work at the old "Clark Brothers Pottery." She married Andrew Jackson Nichols from Bowling Green, Ky. Died February 19, 1912 at Cannelton, Ind.

Lucinda Elizabeth Wood- Sent to Louisville, Ky., then to Smithfield, Ky., where she married James Williamson Shelly on December 23, 1866. She moved to Louisville, Ky., then to Effingham, Ill., then to Ball Ground, Ga. in 1886. In 1910 she moved to Cartersville, Ga., where she died on December 5, 1918.

Margarette Wood- Sent to Louisville, Ky. where she died. The death occurred in 1864 while two men were carrying her in a chair. Margarette was Lucinda's mother.

Mary Ann Sumner- Died on the trip north to Louisville, Ky. She was Lucinda's grandmother.

Easter Wood- Sent to Louisville and married a man named Merritt in Louisville. She died after having two children and is buried in Louisville, Ky.

The Bryant Family- Sent to Louisville, Ky. and settled in Cannelton, Ind.

John N. Brown- Sent to Louisville, Ky. and then to Indianapolis, Ind., after the war moved to Atlanta, Ga.

Mary Brown- Sent to Louisville, Ky. and then to Indianapolis, Ind. After the war, she moved to Atlanta, Ga. with her husband John.

Olney Eldredge- Superintendent of the Roswell Cotton Mills was sent to Louisville, Ky. It is known Olney did return to Roswell as many accounts are written of him in Cobb County Newspapers, after the war. The accounts are of his current work at the Roswell Cotton Mill or of his health.

Theophile Roche- Sent north to Louisville, Ky. but never arrived. At a station between Chattanooga, Tn. and Nashville, Tn., he left the mill hands. He went to New York and then to No 12 Rue Clery Paris, France. He sued the United States Government for $120,000 in the early 1880's, over the burning of the woolen mill. The lawsuit was dismissed on July 2, 1883 for want of prosecution. Theophile was born in Eureux, France on September 3, 1818.

The information on the Kendley family came from George Kendley of Marietta, Ga., a descendant.

The information on the Wood and Sumner family came from Wayne Shelly of Rome, Ga., a descendant.

The Bryant family information came from a March 19, 1943 newspaper in Cannelton, Indiana, *The Cannelton Telephone*.

The information on John Brown, Mary Brown, and Theophile Roche came from documents in the French and American claim commission.

The information on Olney Eldredge came from William King's diary, and Cobb County newspapers printed after the civil war.

Mary Kendley May
Courtesy of George H. Kendley

Appendix B

The following is known information on the U.S. personnel killed during the lightning storm of July 14, 1864.

1st Sgt. John Pratt; 2 U.S. Artillery Battery F, 16th Army Corps, 4th Division. Present interment: The Marietta Georgia National Cemetery. Sec. M, Grave 4451

Pvt. Thomas Smith; 2 U.S. Artillery Battery F, 16th Army Corps, 4th Division. Present interment: The Marietta Georgia National Cemetery. Sec. F, Grave 4727.

Bugler John Felker; 2 U.S. Artillery Battery F, 16th Army Corps, 4th Division. Present interment: The Marietta Georgia National Cemetery, Sec. M, Grave 4452.

Corpl. Osborn Wilson; 4th Michigan Cavalry, Co. A., 2nd Division, 1st Brigade. Present interment: The Marietta Georgia National Cemetery, Sec. F, Grave 5015.

Pvt. John Hensil; 18th Missouri Infantry, Company I, 16th Army Corps, 4th Division , 1st Brigade. Present interment: The Marietta Georgia National Cemetery, Sec. F, Grave 5010.

Pvt. Stanislans Firmback; 2nd Missouri Artillery, Battery F, 15th Army Corps, 1st Division. Present interment: Unknown.

P. Thomas (Black, Male); Pioneer Corps, 16th Army Corps, 2nd Division. Present interment: The Marietta Georgia National Cemetery, Sec. F, Grave 5113.

Note: A 1869 Government printing, entitled *Roll of Honor,* lists an unknown U.S. soldier's original place of interment at Roswell, Ga. His remains were interred into the Marietta Georgia National Cemetery and is listed as buried in Sec. D, Grave 865. This location is no longer valid as the cemetery graves some unknown years ago, were renumbered. Another U.S. Soldier, by the name of Red_____, J.R., is reported as originally interred at Roswell. He is presently buried in Sec. F, Grave 5016. The identity of this soldier's unit is presently unknown.

Corporal John W. Taylor and P. Thomas head markers are currently marked as unknowns.

Appendix C

Known Union casualties in the Roswell area.

Pvt. Mason Bryant; 48th Illinois Infantry, Co. B, 15th Army Corps, 4th Division, 3rd Brigade. Present interment: unknown. (Drowned in the Chattahoochee River while bathing July 16, 1864.)

Appendix C

Appendix D

The Roswell area in 1864

Modern map with current street names

Maps by Michael D. Hitt

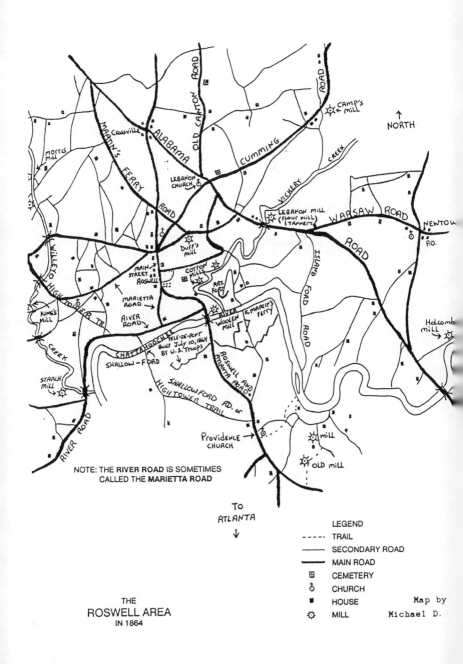

NOTE: THE **RIVER ROAD** IS SOMETIMES
CALLED THE **MARIETTA ROAD**

TO
ATLANTA
↓

THE
ROSWELL AREA
IN 1864

↑
NORTH

LEGEND

```
- - - -   TRAIL
———       SECONDARY ROAD
━━━       MAIN ROAD
⊞         CEMETERY
ᕯ         CHURCH
■         HOUSE
✿         MILL
```

Map by
Michael D.

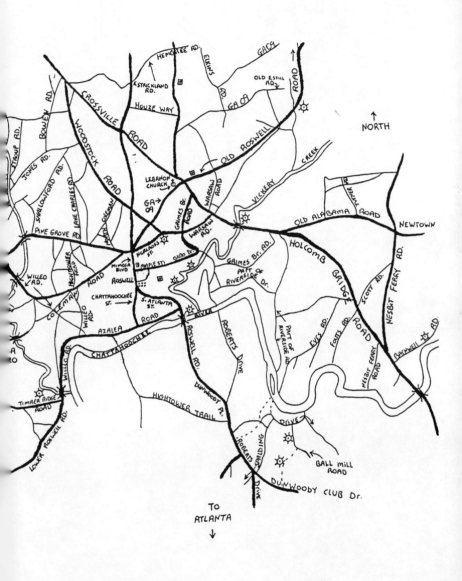

MODERN MAP
WITH
CURRENT STREET NAMES

Map by
Michael D. Hitt

Endnotes

1. Confederate War Records of the Roswell Battalion [Georgia Department of Archives and History]
2. Major George B. Davis, Leslie J. Perry, Joseph W. Kirkley, *War of the Rebellion*; [Washington, Government Printing Office, 1891], ser. 1, Vol.. 38, pt. 4, p. 727.
3. Personal letter written by Barrington King to Rev. W.E. Baker dated May 30, 1864.
4. Testimony in A.S. Atkinson & others Executors of the estate of Charles McDonald Dec. vs. A.V. Brumby & W.J. Russell in May of 1869, to the Superior Court of Fulton Co., State of Georgia.
5. O.R. Ser. 1, Vol. 38, pt. 4, pp. 770-771.
6. Personal letter written by Captain W.H. Clark to Ralph King dated July 3, 1864.
7. O.R. Ser. 1, Vol. 38, pt. 5, pp. 48-49.
8. Sgt. Benjamin F. Mager, *72nd Indiana Regiment*, [1882],   p. 332.
9. S.A. Jordon, *Diary of Pvt. Stephen A. Jordon 9th Regiment Tennessee Cavalry CSA.*, p. 21.
10. Testimony in A.S. Atkinson & Others Executors of the estate of Charles McDonald dec. vs. A.V. Brumby & W.J. Russell in May of 1869, to the Superior Court of Fulton Co., State of Georgia.
11. O.R. Ser. 1, Vol. 38, pt. 5, p. 60.

12. Captain Joseph G. Vale, *Minty and the Cavalry* [Edwin K. Meyer, Printer and Binder, 1886], p. 321.
13. John A. Nourse, *History of The Chicago Board of Trade Battery,* [July 22, 1862 to July 3, 1865], p. 88.
14. Captain Joseph G. Vale, pp. 821-822.
15. The French and American Claims Commission, Theophile Roche vs. The United States, 1884-85, National Archives, Washington, D.C.
16. O.R. Ser. 1, Vol. 38, pt. 5, p. 69.
17. John A. Nourse, p. 88.
18. Personal letter written by Pvt. Silas C. Stevens of The Chicago Board of Trade Battery.
19. O.R. Ser. 1, Vol. 38, pt. 5, p. 68.
20. John A. Nourse, pp. 88-89.
21. O.R. Ser. 1, Vol. 38, pt. 5, pp. 76-77.
22. O.R. Ser. 1, Vol. 38, pt. 5, pp. 75-76.
23. French and American Claims Commission, *Theophile Roche' vs. United States,* Statement of John N. Brown on October 27, 1882 to Commissioner J. C. Jenkins, National Archives, Washington, D.C.
24. Sgt. Benjamin F. Mager, p. 333.
25. Ibid, p. 333.
26. O.R. Ser. 1, Vol. 38, pt. 5, p. 870.
27. O.R. Ser. 1, Vol. 38, pt. 5, pp. 869-870.
28. O.R. Ser. 1, Vol. 38, pt. 1, p. 896.
29. Sgt. Benjamin F. Mager, p. 334.
30. John A. Nourse, p. 89.
31. Sgt. Benjamin F. Mager, pp. 334-335.
32. John A. Nourse, p. 89.
33. Sgt. Benjamin F. Mager, p. 335.
34. O.R. Ser. 1, Vol. 38, pt. 1, p. 851.
35. Captain Joseph G. Vale, pp. 322-323.
36. Sgt. Benjamin F. Mager, pp. 335-336.
37. John A. Nourse, p. 89.
38. O.R. Ser. 1, Vol. 38, pt. 5, p. 100.
39. Sgt. Benjamin F. Mager, p. 337.
40. Ibid, p. 337.

41. *A History of the Seventy-third Regiment of Illinois Infantry Volunteers,* copyright 1890, p. 319.
42. Captain John W. Tuttle, *Diary of John W. Tuttle Captain Co. G. 3rd Ky Inf. Vol.,* p. 48.
43. O.R. Ser. 1, Vol. 38, pt. 5, p. 92.
44. Ibid, pp. 92-93.
45. Captain John W. Tuttle, pp. 48-49.
46. Ibid, p. 49.
47. *A History of the Seventy-third Regiment of Illinois Infantry Volunteers,* p. 319.
48. Sgt. Benjamin F. Mager, pp. 336-337.
49. O.R. Ser. 1, Vol. 38, pt. 5, p. 100.
50. Captain John W. Tuttle, p. 49.
51. Frederick C. Cross, *Nobly They Served The Union,* The Civil War Letters and Diary of Lieut. Col. Henry Granville Stratton, Arranged and Edited by Frederick C. Cross, Copyright 1976, p. 102.
52. O.R. Ser. 1, Vol. 38, pt. 2, p. 838.
53. Sgt. Benjamin F. Mager, pp. 337-339.
54. *A History of the Seventy-third Regiment of Illinois Infantry Volunteers,* p. 319.
55. O.R. Ser. 1, Vol. 38, pt. 1, p. 337.
56. W.H. Chamberlin, Late Major of the Regiment, *History of the Eighty-first Regiment Ohio Infantry Volunteers during the War of the Rebellion,* 1865.
57. James P. Snell, *Diary of James P. Snell,* [July 9 to July 18, 1864] pp. 8-9.
58. Pvt. John Ginste, *Diary of John Ginste,* [July 8 to July 16, 1864] p. 10.
59. O.R. Ser. 1, Vol. 38, pt. 5, p. 109.
60. Captain John W. Tuttle, p. 49.
61. Captain Joseph G. Vale, pp. 323-334.
62. James P. Snell, pp. 8-9.
63. O.R. Ser. 1, Vol. 38, pt. 5, p. 104.
64. Ibid, p. 104.
65. William King, *Diary of William King Cobb County, Georgia July 2, to September 9, 1864,* pp. 8-10.

66. O.R. Ser. 1, Vol. 38, pt. 5, p. 874.
67. O.R. Ser. 1, Vol. 38, pt. 5, p. 109.
68. O.R. Ser. 1, Vol. 38, pt. 2, p. 838.
69. Letters of Pvt. George Hovey Cadman of the 39th Ohio Infantry to Esther Cooper Cadman, July 15, 1864, p. 272.
70. Margaret Brobst Roth, *Well Mary,* The Civil War Letters of Pvt. John F. Brobst, Edited by Margaret Brobst Roth, p. 73.
71. Captain John W. Tuttle, p. 49.
72. *A History of the Seventy-third Regiment of Illinois Infantry Volunteers,* p. 320.
73. Sgt. Benjamin F. Mager, p. 338.
74. James P. Snell, pp. 9-10.
75. O.R. Ser. 1, Vol. 38, pt. 5, p. 118.
76. O.R. Ser. 1, Vol. 38, pt. 5, p. 119.
77. Pvt. John Ginste, p. 10.
78. Letters of Pvt. John F. Brobst, p. 76.
79. Charles Wright, *A Corporal's Story Company C, 81st O. V.I.,* copyright 1887, p. 123.
80. Sgt. Benjamin F. Mager, p. 339.
81. Pvt. Jesse B. Luce, *Diary of Pvt. Jesse B. Luce Co. B. 125th Ohio Inf.,* p. 14.
82. O.R. Ser. 1, Vol. 38, pt. 2, p. 838.
83. Personal Letter Written by Lt. George Hurlburt of the 14th Ohio Battery, to Angie, Dated July 11, 1864, p. 30.
84. Captain John W. Tuttle, p. 49.
85. John A. Nourse, p. 89.
86. Sgt. Benjamin F. Mager, p. 339.
87. Oscar O. Winther, *With Sherman to the Sea,* The Civil War letters, Diaries & Reminiscences of Theodore F. Upson, edited by Oscar Osburn Winther, Copyright 1943, p. 119.
88. Lt. George Hurlburt Letter, p. 31.
89. John A. Nourse, p. 90.
90. G.M. Armstrong, *Reminiscences of the Civil War,* from Diaries of members of the 103rd Illinois Volunteer Infantry, Copyright 1904, pp. 99-100.

91. Thaddeus H. Capron, *Diary of Thaddeus H. Capron 15th Illinois Infantry*, p. 386.
92. W.L. Curry, *Diary of W.L. Curry, First Ohio Cavalry*, p. 172.
93. O.R. Ser. 1, Vol. 38, pt. 3, p. 383.
94. O.R. Ser. 1, Vol. 38, pt. 5, p. 139.
95. *Diary of a Member of Company D. 12th Indiana, 1st Brigade, 4th Division, 15th Army Corps*, p. 20.
96. Sgt. Benjamin F. Mager, p. 340.
97. John A. Nourse, p. 90.
98. William King, p. 14.
99. James P. Snell, pp. 11-12.
100. O.R. Ser. 1, Vol. 38, pt. 3, p. 53.
101. Letters of Pvt. George H. Cadman, p. 273.
102. *Cincinnati Commercial*, July 21, 1864 quoting a July 17, 1864 article from the *New York Tribune*, about an incident which occurred July 15, 1864.
103. G.M. Armstrong, p. 100.
104. Letters of Pvt. George H. Cadman. p. 273.
105. 12th Indiana Infantry, p. 20.
106. Sgt. Benjamin F. Mager, pp. 340-341.
107. John A. Nourse, p. 90.
108. James P. Snell, p. 12.
109. 12th Indiana Infantry, p. 20.
110. William M. Anderson, *We Are Shermans Men. The Letters of Henry Orendorff*, Copyright 1986, p. 95.
111. R. Willey, *I Soldiered for the Union*, The Civil War Diary of William Bluffton Miller, Company K, 75th Indiana Volunteer Infantry, Edited by R. Willey, p. 174.
112. O.R. Ser. 1, Vol. 38, pt. 5, p. 155.
113. James P. Snell, p. 14.
114. O.R. Ser. 1, Vol. 38, pt. 5, pp. 156-157.
115. G.M. Armstrong, p. 101.
116. James P. Snell, pp. 14-15.
117. Ibid, p. 15.
118. H. Henry Speer, *Diary of Henry Speer, 78th Ohio Volunteer Infantry, 17th Army Corps*, p. 21.
119. O.R. Ser. 1, Vol. 38, pt. 5, p. 885.

120. William King, July 17, 1864.
121. John A. Nourse, p. 90.
122. O.R. Ser. 1, Vol. 38, pt. 5, p. 889.
123. John A. Nourse, pp. 90-91.
124. O.R. Ser. 1., Vol. 38, pt. 5, p. 209.
125. *Nashville Times*, July 20, 1864.
126. O.R. Ser. 1, Vol. 38, pt. 5, pp. 218-219.
127. O.R. Ser. 1, Vol. 38. pt. 5, p. 221.
128.*New York Tribune,* July 21, 1864, p. 1.
129. *New York Times,* July 21, 1864.
130. *Louisville Daily Journal*, July 21, 1864.
131. O.R. Ser. 1, Vol. 38, pt. 5, p. 238.
132. O.R. Ser. 1, Vol. 38, pt. 5, p. 239.
133. O.R. Ser. 1, Vol. 38, pt. 5, p. 242.
134. O.R. Ser. 1, Vol. 38, pt. 5, p. 243.
135. O.R. Ser. 1, Vol. 38, pt. 5, pp. 251-252.
136. O.R. Ser. 1, Vol. 38, pt. p. 252.
137. *Elk Horn Independent,* August 10, 1864, p. 3.
138. John A. Nourse, p. 93.
139. *New York Times*, July 27, 1864, p. 2.
140. *Patriot and Union*, July 27, 1864.
141. William King, July 27, 1864.
142. Roswell Battalion, Confederate War Records, Georgia Department of Archives and History, Atlanta, Georgia.
143. O.R. Ser. 1, Vol. 39, pt. 2, p. 210.
144. Ibid, pp. 210-211.
145. O.R. Ser. 1. Vol. 38, pt. 5, p. 327.
146. O.R. Ser. 1, Vol. 38, pt. 5, p. 330.
147. *Patriot and Union*, August 2, 1864.
148. O.R. Ser. 1, Vol. 38, pt. 2, p. 918.
149. Ibid, p. 918.
150. O.R. Ser. 1, Vol. 38, pt. 5, p. 363.
151. *Patriot and Union,* July 4, 1864.
152. O.R. Ser. 1, Vol. 38, pt. 5, p. 388.
153. O.R. Ser. 1, Vol. 38, pt. 5, p. 388.
154. William King, August 5, 1864.
155. O.R. Ser. 1, Vol. 38, pt. 5, p. 406.

156. Ibid, p. 417.
157. Ibid, p. 417.
158. O.R. Ser. 1, Vol. 7, Prisoners of War, etc., p. 563.
159. *Atlanta Magazine, The Roswell Women,* 1982, by Barbara Thomas, p. 85.
160. O.R. Ser. 1, Vol. 38, pt. 5, p. 420.
161. *Louisville Daily Journal,* August 9, 1864.
162. O.R. Ser. 2, Vol. 5, Prisoners of War, etc., p. 682.
163. *Louisville Daily Journal,* August 10, 1864.
164. William King, August 10, 1864.
165. O.R. Ser. 1, Vol. 38, pt. 5, pp. 486-487.
166. O.R. Ser. 1, Vol. 38, pt. 5, p. 488.
167. O.R. Ser. 1, Vol. 38, pt. 5, p. 489.
168. O.R. Ser. 1, Vol. 38, pt. 5, p. 574.
169. *Nashville Daily Press & Times,* August 20, 1864, p. 2.
170. William King, August 22, 1864.
171. O.R. Ser. 1, Vol. 38, pt. 5, p. 640.
172. *Louisville Daily Journal,* August 23, 1864.
173. William King, August 24, 1864.
174. *Louisville Daily Journal,* August 24, 1864.
175. O.R. Ser. 1, Vol. 38, pt. 5, p. 671.
176. *Patriot and Union,* August 27, 1864.
177. William King, August 27, 1864.
178. O.R. Ser. 1, Vol. 38, pt. 5, p. 691-692.
179. William King, September 1, 1864.
180. *Southern Watchman,* July 28, 1864.
181. O.R. Ser. 1, Vol. 38, pt. 5, p. 763.
182. O.R. Ser. 1, Vol. 47, pt. 2, p. 1152.
183. O.R. Ser. 1, Vol. 38, pt. 5, p. 796.
184. *New York Commercial,* September 9, 1864.
185. *The Atlanta Journal,* Magazine Section, February 28, 1932, p. 6.
186. Major Williams, *Diary of Major Matthew J. Williams,* September 18, 1864, p. 9.
187. O.R. Ser. 1, Vol. 39, pt. 2, p. 444.
188. *Mary Walker Papers,* Syracuse University Library, New York.

189. *Louisville Daily Journal*, September 23, 1864.
190. Jno. Robertson, *Michigan in the War,* compiled by Jno. Robertson, 1882, p. 85.
191. O.R. Ser. 1, Vol. 39, pt. 2, p. 506.
192. O.R. Ser. 1, Vol. 39, pt. 2, p. 520.
193. O.R. Ser. 1, Vol. 39, pt. 3, p. 47.
194. O.R. Ser. 1, Vol. 39, pt. 3, p. 321.
195. National Archives Regimental Records of the 9th Michigan Cavalry, Month of October, 1864.
196. O.R. Ser. 1, Vol. 39, pt. 1, p. 684.
197. O.R. Ser. 1, Vol. 39, pt. 1, p. 584.
198. Letter from Rev. Pratt to Col. Barrington S. King, December 15, 1864.
199. C.W. Faulkner letter, from Camp Douglas Military Prison, January 1, 1865.
200. *Mary Walker Papers*, Syracuse University Library, New York.
201. O.R. Ser. 1, Vol. 8, Prisoners of War, etc., p. 261.
202. Ibid, p. 261.
203. *Mary Walker Papers*, Syracuse University Library, New York.
204. *Louisville Daily Journal*, May 1865.
205. *In And Out Of The Lines*, Frances Thomas Howard, 1905, p. 80.
206. Barrington King letter to Eva, June 7, 1865.
207. Minutes of the Roswell Manufacturing Company, [1840-1899], July 19, 1865.
208. *The Atlanta Journal*, Magazine Section, February 28, 1932, p. 6.
209. O.R. Ser. 3, Vol. 5, p. 587.
210. Barrington King Letter to Ralph King, July 22, 1865.

Bibliography

Books

Anderson, William M. *We Are Sherman's Men: The Letters of Henry Orendorff.* Macomb, Illinois: Western Illinois University, 1986.

Armstrong, G.M., Newton Ellis, C.F. Matteson, H.H. Orendorff, S.R. Quigley, A.J. Stutes. *Reminiscences of the Civil War from Diaries of Members of the 103rd Illinois Volunteer Infantry.* Chicago, Illinois: Press of J.F. Leaming & Co., 1904.

Chamberlin, W.H.. *History of the Eighty-first Regiment Ohio Infantry Volunteers During the War of the Rebellion.* Cincinnati, Ohio: Gazette Steam Printing House, 1865.

Confederate War Records of the Roswell Battalion 1863-1864. [Georgia Department of Archives and History, Atlanta, Georgia.]

Cross, Frederick C. *Nobly They Served The Union: The Civil War Letters and Diary of Lieut. Col. Henry Granville Stratton.* Privately published: 1976.

Curry, W.L. *Four Years in the Saddle: History of the First Regiment, Ohio Cavalry.* Columbus, Ohio: Champlin Printing Co., 1898.

Davis, Major George B., Leslie J. Perry, Joseph W. Kirkley. *War of the Rebellion: A compilation of the Official Records of*

Union and Confederate Armies. Washington, D.C.: Government Printing Office, 1891.

Howard, Frances Thomas. *In And Out Of The Lines,* New York and Washington: The Neale Publishing Company,1905.

Mager, Sergeant Benjamin F. *Seventy-second Indiana Regiment.* 1882. [Georgia Department of Archives & History, Atlanta, Georgia.]

Newlin, W.H. *A History of the Seventy-third Regiment of Illinois Infantry Volunteers.* Privately published: 1890.

Milhollen, Hirst Dillon. *Horsemen Blue and Gray: A Pictoral History.* New York: Oxford University Press, 1960.

Miller, Francis Trevelyan. *The Photographic History of the Civil War: The Decisive Battles.* New York: Castle Books, 1957.

North to Antietam: Battles and Leaders of the Civil War. New York: Castle Books, 1956.

Regimental Records of the Ninth Michigan Cavalry, Month of October, 1864. [National Archives, Washington, D.C.]

Robertson, Jno. *Michigan in the War.* Lansing, Michigan: W.S. George & Co., State Printers and Binders, 1882.

Roth, Margaret Brobst. *Well Mary: The Civil War Letters of Private John F. Brobst.* Madison, Wisconsin: The University of Wisconsin Press, 1960.

Sunderland, Glenn W. *Wilder's Lightning Brigade...and Its Spencer Repeaters.* Washington, Illinois: The Book Works, 1984.

Vale, Joseph G. *Minty and the Cavalry.* Harrisburg, Pennsylvania: Edwin K. Meyers, Printer and Binder, 1886.

Warner, Ezra J. *Generals in Blue: Lives of the Union Commanders.* Baton Rouge, Louisiana: Louisiana State University Press, 1964.

Warner, Ezra J. *Generals in Gray: Lives of the Confederate Commanders.* Baton Rouge, Louisiana: Louisiana State University Press, 1959.

Willey, R. *I Soldiered for the Union: The Civil War Diary of William Bluffton Miller.* Privately published: n.d.

Winther, Oscar O. *With Sherman to the Sea: The Civil War Letters, Diaries & Reminiscences of Theodore F. Upson.* Baton Rouge, Louisiana: Louisiana State Press, 1943.

Wright, Charles. *A Corporal's Story: Experiences in the Ranks of Co. C, 81 Ohio, During the War for the Maintenance of the Union. 1861-1864.* Philadelphia, Pennsylvania: James Beale Printer, 1887.

Diaries

Capron, Thaddeus H. *Diary of Thaddeus H. Capron, Fifteenth Illinois Infantry. N.: n.p., n.d.*

Diary of a Member of Company D, Twelfth Indiana, First Brigade, Fourth Division, Fifteenth Army Corps. N.: n.p., n.d.

Ginste, John. *Diary of John Ginste.* N: n.p., n.d.

Jordon, S.A. *Diary of Private Stephen A. Jordon, Ninth Regiment Tennessee Cavalry C.S.A.* N.: n.p., n.d.

King, William. *Diary of William King, Cobb County, Georgia.* N.: n.p., n.d. [University of North Carolina at Chapel Hill, N.C.]

Luce, Jesse B. *Diary of Private Jesse B. Luce, Company B, 125th Ohio Infantry.* N.: n.p., n.d.

Minutes of the Roswell Manufacturing Company, 1840-1899, July 19, 1865. [Dekalb Historical Society Library, Decatur, Georgia.]

Nourse, John A. *History of the Chicago Board of Trade Battery, July 22, 1862 to July 3, 1865.* N.: n.p., n.d. [Chicago Historical Society Library, Chicago, Illinois.]

Speer, Henry., *Diary of Henry Speer, Seventy-eighth Ohio Volunteer Infantry, Seventeenth Army Corps.* N.: n.p., n.d.

Snell, James P. *Diary of James P. Snell.* N.: n.p., n.d.

Tuttle, John W. *Diary of John W. Tuttle, Captain of Company G, Third Kentucky Volunteer Infantry.* N.: n.p., n.d.

Williams, Matthew J. *Diary of Major Matthew J. Williams.* N.: n.p., n.d.

Legal Papers

The French and American Claims Commission, Theophile Roche vs. The United States, 1884-1885, National Archives, Washington, D.C.

Testimony in A.S. Atkinson & Others, Executors of the estate of Charles McDonald Dec. vs. A.V. Brumby & W.J. Russell in May of 1869, to the Superior Court of Fulton County, State of Georgia.

Letters

A Brief History of the Roswell Battalion of Cobb County, Georgia. F.P.P., 1865 [Barrington King Collection, Georgia Department of Archives & History.]

Letters of Private George Hovey Cadman of the Thirty-ninth Ohio Infantry, to Esther Cooper Cadman, 1864.

Personal letter written by Captain W.H. Clark to Ralph King, July 3, 1864.

Letter by C.W. Faulkner from Camp Douglas Military Prison, January 1, 1865.

Personal letter written by Lieutenant George Hurlburt of the Fourteenth Ohio Battery, to Angie, July 11, 1864.

Personal letter written by Barrington King to Rev. W.E. Baker, May 30, 1864.

Personal letter written by Barrington King to Eva, June 7, 1865.

Personal letter written by Barrington King to Ralph King, July 22, 1865.

Personal letter written by Rev. Pratt to Colonel Barrington S. King, December 15, 1864.

Personal letter written by Private Silas C. Stevens of the Chicago Board of Trade Battery, July 6, 1864.

Mary Walker Papers, Syracuse University Library, New York.

Periodicals

Atlanta Magazine, "The Roswell Women." Barbara Thomas 1982.

The Atlanta Journal, Magazine Section. February 28, 1932. Atlanta, Georgia.

Cincinnati Commercial, July 21, 1864, quoting a July 17, 1864 article from the *New York Tribune* about an incident which occurred July 15, 1864. Cincinnati, Ohio.

Elk Horn Independent, August 10, 1864. Wisconsin.

Frank Leslie's Illustrated Newspaper, 1864.

Harper's Weekly, August, 1864.

Louisville Daily Journal, July 21, 1864, August 9, 1864, August 10, 1864, May, 1865. Louisville, Kentucky.

Nashville Daily Press & Times, August 10, 1864. Nashville, Tennessee.

Nashville Daily Times and *True Union*, July 20, 1864. Nashville, Tennessee.

New York Commercial, September 9, 1864. New York.

New York Times, July 21, 1864; July 27, 1864. New York.

New York Tribune, July 21, 1864. New York.

Patriot and Union, July 1864; July 27, 1864; August 2, 1864. Harrisburg, Pennsylvania.

Southern Watchman, July 28, 1864. Athens, Georgia.

Index

S

Sherman's army reaches

WASHINGTON, Dec. 21, 1864—Union Gen. William T. Sherman today presented the city of Savannah to President Abraham Lincoln as a Christmas gift.

Sherman's troops entered the important Georgia port city yesterday after a 10-day siege. Today the President received a telegram from the general calling the victory a Christmas present.

The Union forces took Savannah on a drive to the sea only 25 days after leaving Atlanta. The march cut a wide path through this Confederate stronghold from west to east. Sherman's troops moved rapidly on a 60-mile-wide front. On the general's orders they destroyed and plundered the farming country, which was a principal source of supply for the Confederate forces.

The troops carried no provisions, but lived off the land. They destroyed what they could not use, as part of the Union effort to starve the Confederacy into surrendering. Sherman used the same tactics last spring and summer on his drive from Chattanooga, Tenn., to Atlanta.

The general forced the Confederates out of Atlanta on Sept. 1. Six weeks later

he set out for Savannah. Confe leaders were expecting him to ret the north instead, so the drive me little opposition from southern n units.

Troops of Confederate Gen. J Hood, whom Sherman had defea

Gen. Sherman's armies captu